CW01368371

The Seven Sacred Flames

Aurelia Louise Jones

Mount Shasta Light Publishing

The Seven Sacred Flames

ISBN 978-0-9700902-8-7

© Copyright 2007 by Aurelia Louise Jones

English Publication - June 2007

Mount Shasta Light Publishing
PO Box 1509
Mount Shasta CA 96067-1509
USA

Phone: 530-926-4599
Fax: 530-926-4159

E-mail: aurelia@mslpublishing.com
Web Site: www.mslpublishing.com
Also: www.lemurianconnection.com

All rights reserved

Graphics of Masters and Chakras: Marius Michael-George
www.MariusFineArt.com

Cover Design: Aaron Rose

Page Layout and Formatting: Aaron Rose

Printed in China through Global PSD

Table of Contents

Dedication vii
Acknowledgements viii
Preface xi
Introduction x
Foreword xii
   The Judge—The One Who Embodies Universal LAW! xvii
   Lord Maitreya: The Planetary Christ xx
   The Planetary Spiritual Hierarchy and Beyond xxii

The Seven Sacred Flames

The First Ray: The Flame of the Will of God 3
   About Master El Morya 4
   Embodiments of El Morya.. 4
   Temple of Good Will 5
   Transmission from Beloved El Morya 6
   Prayer for First Ray Healing: God's Will Prayer 13
   Discourse from Adama with Master El Morya 14
   Meditation: Journey to the Will of God Temple 32

The Second Ray: The Flame of Illumination and Wisdom 37
   About Lord Lanto, Teacher of Ancient Wisdom.............. 38
   Embodiments of Lord Lanto.. 39
   Royal Teton Retreat 39
   Transmission from Beloved Lord Lanto........................ 41
   Message from Master Kuthumi 44
   Prayer for Second Ray Healing: Illumination and Peace .. 47
   Discourse from Adama with Lord Lanto 48
   Meditation: Journey to the Illumination Temple 58

The Third Ray: The Flame of Cosmic Love 65
   About Paul the Venetian, Chohan of the Ray of Love 66
   Embodiments of Paul the Venetian 67

The Chateau of Liberty, Retreat of Paul the Venetian......67
  Transmission from Paul the Venetian..........................68
  Tips for Regaining your Immortality 72
  Prayer for Third Ray Healing: I Open My Cup to Thee 75
  Discourse from Adama with Paul the Venetian................76
  Codes of Conduct for a Disciple of the Holy Spirit..........86
  Meditation: Journey to the Temple of Love 88

The Fourth Ray: The Ascension Flame................................95
  About Lord Serapis Bey 96
  Embodiments of Lord Serapis Bey...............................96
  The Temple of Luxor..97
  Transmission from Lord Serapis Bey..........................101
  Prayer for Fourth Ray Healing: Personal Ascension 105
  Discourse from Adama with Serapis Bey 106
  Meditation: Journey to the Ascension Temple 116
  The Atomic Accelerator/Ascension Chair 120
  How to Create Your Ceremony 125

The Fifth Ray: The Flame of Healing 131
  About Master Hilarion.. 132
  Embodiments of Master Hilarion 132
  The Temple of Truth 133
  About Healing 134
  The Body Elemental 136
  Transmission from Beloved Hilarion........................137
  Prayer for Third Ray Healing 143
  Discourse from Adama with Master Hilarion............... 144
  Meditation: Journey to the Great Jade Temple 156

The Sixth Ray: The Flame of Resurrection 159
  About Lady Nada and Lord Sananda 162
  Lord Sananda, Initiator of the Christian Dispensation...163
  Embodiments of Lord Sananda............................... 165
  Embodiments of Lady Nada 166

Table of Contents

    Retreats of the Masters of the Sixth Ray 167
    Message of Love from Lord Sananda and Lady Nada 169
    Invocation to the Flame of Resurrection 175
    Discourse from Adama with Jesus/Sananda and Nada .. 176
    Meditation: Journey to the Temple of Resurrection 191

The Seventh Ray: The Violet Flame of Transmutation 197
    The Home of Master Saint Germain 198
    Embodiments of Master Saint Germain 198
    Excerpts from Lord Zadkiel 198
    Transmission from Beloved Saint Germain 202
    Invocation to the Violet Flame: Mantle of Violet Fire ... 207
    Discourse from Adama with Master Saint Germain 208
    Invocation to the Violet Flame 212
    Meditation: Journey to the Violet Flame Temple 224

Prayers and Invocations to the First Ray 229
    The Prayer of Surrender 229
    For a Forcefield of Protection 230
Prayers and Invocations to the Second Ray 231
    Call to the Illumination Flame 231
    Invocation to the Sun 231
Prayers and Invocations to the Third Ray 232
    Adoration to Your God Presence 232
    Prayer for Divine Love 232
Prayers and Invocations to the Fourth Ray 234
    Prayer for Self-Love and Ascension 234
    Ascension Affirmations by Archangel Gabriel 235
Prayers and Invocations to the Fifth Ray 236
    Healing Through Releasing Negative Energies 236
    Prayer to Request Miracles 237
    I Now Accept My Abundance 238
Prayers and Invocations to the Sixth Ray 239
    Resurrection Affirmation 239
    Prayer of Saint Francis 240

Prayers and Invocations to the Seventh Ray 241
    Invocation to the Violet Flame 241
    Flood the Earth with Violet Fire 242

About Aurelia Louise Jones 243
Note from Aurelia Louise Jones 244
Telos World-Wide Foundation 245
Mount Shasta Light Publishing Publications 246

Dedication

It is my honor and privilege to dedicate this book to all the Masters of Wisdom of this planetary hierarchy and to the entire spirit of the Great White Brotherhood. This material is published as a tribute and in deep gratitude for the Ascended Masters' relentless devotion, patience, love and determination in assisting each of us individually and all of humanity on Earth to move beyond the long dark night that we have all endured for so long.

This vast wealth of information and wisdom the Masters have shared with us, especially in the last 100 years, has truly prepared us for the great awakening that is now taking place for the Ascension of Earth and humanity.

I also dedicate this book in gratitude to Adama, Ahnahmar and the Lemurian Brotherhood of Light of Telos who have kept the Ascension Flame burning bright on behalf of surface dwellers for the last 12,000 years, and continue to do so until we gain enough maturity and mastery, as a race, to do it for ourselves.

Acknowledgements

I wish to express my deep gratitude to all my friends around the world who have supported my work and the emergence of the Lemurian Mission. I also thank the various publishers for making the Telos material available in their own countries and languages.

I express my deepest gratitude for the members of the Telos World Wide Foundation in Montreal who have worked tirelessly in creating the structures that need to be in place in preparation for the huge expansion in human consciousness expected to take place between now and year 2012. I thank especially Line Ouellet, the president of the foundation, who has volunteered her time, many hours a week for the last four years, in order to assure the success and the continuation of the work and role the Telos World Wide Foundation is destined to accomplish worldwide, as humanity awakens to their divine potential.

I also want to thank Gaston Tempelmann, president of Telos-France, who works diligently to assist and prepare the expansion of the Lemurian Mission in France and Europe now and in the years to come.

Acknowledgements

Without all of you, the miracles of Love which now manifest through the reconnection with our Telosian family and the preparation for their emergence among us, could not take place in the wondrous ways it is presently taking place. Those of us who are firmly engaged in this work feel more and more the tangible quality of their love and constant support. To all of you, I express my deepest gratitude and eternal friendship.

It is well indicated for me to mention the teachings of the Masters of Wisdom channeled through Geraldine Innocenti between the years 1950 and 1959. During that time, Geraldine, twin flame of Master El Morya, covered approximately 15,000 pages of original dictations from various Ascended Masters through the Bridge to Freedom dispensation. Her channeling abilities were remarkable! The Ascended Masters brought to humanity a wealth of information and wisdom through her gifted abilities. The teachings given through the messengers Guy Ballard and Geraldine Innocenti in the first part of the 20th century are really ONE. They cannot be separated as they originated from the same source, complementing each other. Some information in this book, such as the description of the various retreats, come from the teachings of the Bridge to Freedom dispensation.

The Seven Sacred Flames

Preface

In the Light and Love of our Creator, we greet you today. It is with much joy in our hearts that we bring you the knowledge of the Sacred Flames. The material herein presents you with an opportunity to increase your understanding of the Ascended Masters' teachings. For those of you who will attune yourself to the vibration of each ray and of each master, you will initiate in your consciousness a personal experience with the Chohan and the Brotherhood serving on the ray you are connecting with. We invite you to gather with us as you read our words and as you connect with the invisible words written between the lines that speak directly to your heart.

We suggest therefore, that each time you begin to read this material, take a quiet moment to go into the secret chamber of your heart to petition a personal experience with the Masters serving on the ray you are contemplating. Do not hesitate to ask for healing, for knowledge and for increased wisdom. As

Preface

you read each chapter, you will feel the presence of the Masters and the vibration of that particular ray. This will give you the opportunity to develop a personal relationship with various ascended beings, enabling you to know them more deeply.

We offer ourselves to you as mentors and guides in your awakening. All of us who speak to you from the pages of this book are members of a large family of Light who love you so dearly. Each step of your awakening presents to you an opportunity for joy and understanding that is unsurpassed in your evolution. It opens for you a door in your own mastery and a seat for you on the ever-expanding council of energies that are guiding the Earth through her own awakening and Ascension. Thank you Aurelia for putting your whole mind, heart and soul into this project.

We are Saint Germain, Adama, and The Judge

Channeled by Catherine Gardner of Mount Shasta

Introduction

The Seven Flames of God for Seven Days

Adama
At this time, I want to give you a short overview of the seven major rays. It would be very beneficial for each of you to focus each day on the energies of one of the seven major rays that flood the planet from Creator Source on that day. All energies of the seven rays flood the planet daily, but each day of the week, one of the rays becomes predominant.

Working with the seven rays in this manner will assist you, in a most profound way, to balance the energies of the seven rays in each one of your chakras throughout your life, and will bring you much greater balance and grace. In the process of ascension and enlightenment, all seven major rays and later on, the five Secret Rays, must be balanced and mastered in order to move on to greater wisdom and mastery in your cosmic future.

In Telos, we work much more effectively each day by amplifying in our hearts, our minds and our daily activities the specific energies of each day of the week. We invite you to experiment with this. You may be pleasantly surprised to discover how much more effectively the energies are amplified and how they assist you.

Sunday, the Yellow Ray of Wisdom, Illumination and the Mind of God is amplified.

Focus on the Mind of God daily in all things, but specifically on Sunday. The Divine Mind will open your own mind to ever expanding Wisdom. True wisdom always comes from the mind of

Introduction

higher perspective and consciousness. As you merge this divine mind with your own, you begin to make decisions and conduct your life in ways that will bring you much ease and satisfaction.

Monday, the Royal Blue Ray of the Will of God is amplified.

Focus on the Will of God for your very life through total surrender to that Divine Will, no matter what your present circumstances appear to be. This is the fastest way to gain your spiritual mastery and freedom. As you align with God's Will, you will notice that your life will manifest more harmony. Bathe your mind, body and soul each day with that energy, and soon, you will reap its many benefits.

Tuesday, the Rose-Pink Ray of Divine Love of God is amplified.

Focus on the transforming and healing influence of the energies of Divine Love. Love is the glue that creates, transforms, heals and harmonizes all things. Take time in your life to breathe it in and merge with this Flame of Divine Love, the key to the power of multiplication and all good things you desire. As you merge with this Flame in a greater measure, limitations start dissolving and you become the master of your destiny.

Wednesday, the Emerald Green Ray of the Divine Flame of Healing, Precipitation and Abundance is amplified.

Focus on the energies of divine healing in all aspects of your life. This is a balancing and soothing energy that will assist you to align the many distortions you have created in your lives. Invoke and visualize this radiant green liquid healing light blazing through all areas where transformation is needed. The

Green Ray also governs the laws of abundance and prosperity. Also invoke the emerald green Flame to pave the way for the manifestation and precipitation of all your physical and spiritual desires.

Thursday, the Golden Ray of the Resurrection Flame is amplified.

Focus on the energies of this Flame for the resurrection and restoration of your inherited divinity. You are a divine being experiencing human life and learning from it. Because you have strayed in consciousness, your divinity has been veiled. As you invoke and merge with the purple and gold energies of the Resurrection Flame, you will start resurrecting all the gifts and attributes of your divinity. Along with the Violet Flame, this wondrous flame prepares you for the final ritual of Ascension, which is the main purpose for your many incarnations on this planet.

Friday, the Pure Dazzling White Ray of Purity of the Ascension Flame is amplified.

Ascension is the alchemical marriage or divine union of your human-self with your I AM Presence through the process of purification of all misqualification of God's energy throughout your many incarnations. Focus on purifying and clearing all negativity, false beliefs, poor attitudes and habits blocking the manifestation of your spiritual mastery. Fill your auric field and every cell of your physical, mental, emotional and etheric bodies with this pure-white dazzling Ascension Flame. In your meditation, do this with all the rays. It is essential for your spiritual progress.

Saturday, the Penetrating Violet Ray of Transmutation and Freedom is amplified.

Introduction

On Saturday, focus on the many tones and frequencies of the Violet Ray which is most magical. The Violet Flame brings the frequency of change, alchemy, freedom from limitations, royalty, diplomacy, comfort and much more. As you fill your auric field and your heart with the wonders of this Flame, its frequency will start clearing from your life the obstacles and karma that are obstructing the way to the realization of your mastery. Use the Violet Fire as much as you can each day, but especially on Saturday when this ray is amplified in a greater way, and it will serve you well.

As you see, my dear friends, all of the rays are important. None of them can be neglected nor put aside. They all work together in perfect harmony to assist the restoration of your soul and your lost paradise. Self-realization and God-mastery come from the diligent application of these Flames. You are the "responsible" architect of your life. These immortal and eternal Flames of God will work for you as you work with them. No one can interfere with your free will and no one can do it for you. Spiritual progress is brought forth as the result of daily application of God's laws, God's energies through the seven main rays, and the clearing of one's karma and emotional body.

Each day, it is most important that you set time aside to do your spiritual work. Invoking the Sacred Flames and their attributes opens the channels to receive deeper understanding of cosmic laws. Breathe, invoke and fill yourself with these wondrous energies. In your meditation, connect with the energy of these Flames as you contact your Divine Essence and your guides, diligently applying what is shown to you. Seek to lift the veil of mortal illusions and reconnect with the magic and power of the original intent of God for your eternal journey into greater purpose and destiny. Our assistance is also available to you for the asking; a simple prayer request from your heart brings us into your forcefield instantly in answer to your call.

Adama

Foreword

The Judge—
The One Who Embodies Universal LAW!

Aurelia

It is my great honor and privilege to present "The Judge" to the people of Earth through my writings. Let me explain in a few words my understanding of who he is. In the last few weeks, with the assistance of Catherine Gardner, who is fully clairvoyant and clairaudient, I had the opportunity and the benefit of receiving the visit and personal instructions from the being who, in all universes, is known as "The Judge."

He explained that He is the Embodiment of the LAW. He is the Law-maker and sees to it that Universal Laws are explicitly honored and obeyed, through Love and surrender to God's Will, for the sake of maintaining Oneness, Peace and Harmony throughout all universes. He also embodies Knowledge and Wisdom. He travels from universe to universe, from galaxy to galaxy and from planet to planet, particularly visiting places where there is a certain amount of discord from rebellious souls who, through disobedience, have separated themselves from the universal and planetary hierarchies and cause dissonance on their planet. His role is to investigate what is going on and make the necessary decisions to re-establish Divine Order.

Though on Earth "free will" has been an experiment, he visits our planet from time to time to evaluate the situation and progress of mankind; he often removes from the planet those souls who refuse, lifetime after lifetime, to live the way of harmlessness and love. Up to now, his identity has never been revealed to those in incarnation in the third dimension, but he is well known by the those of the spiritual hierarchy who govern the workings of our planet. At this time of Earth Ascension, he is here again to evaluate humanity's progress, to give direction to the planetary hierarchy for the administration of justice, to authorize the discipline of certain souls to assist them in aligning with the Light, or to remove souls from this platform of evolution.

While I was working diligently to meet the deadline for the completion of this book for publication, I felt his presence with me almost constantly, like a loving father, directly sustaining my efforts and my energy level. In one of our conversations, he offered to give a message to humanity through this writing, which I am privileged to present with much gratitude for this blessing.

The Judge Speaks

Greetings, children of Earth! It is the first time that I make myself consciously known to the surface dwellers of Earth. I am indeed grateful for this opportunity to share with the readers of this material, not only my Love and Wisdom, but most of all, my energy which fortifies those who, through their obedience to Universal Laws, will connect with my heart.

Understand that these laws do not exist simply to annoy you; they have an important purpose. Without them, the universes would be places of great chaos. These laws, which you need to make yourself familiar with, are what keep the whole cosmos running smoothly, planets harmonious and abundant and humanities experiencing limitlessness, peace, love and true brotherhood. The obedience to these laws keeps you

Foreword

"karma free," and FREE to enjoy your incarnations as divine beings, without the trauma, pain, abuse and chaos that you experience on the surface of the Earth.

When the people of Earth, long ago, decided to put aside the love and wisdom of a benevolent and wise spiritual hierarchy to experience life without any restriction, a distorted concept of "free will," the request was granted by the Godhead as an experiment. The misuse of "free will" quickly became the law of the land, and those who had self-serving agendas took over and enslaved you in more ways than you care to know. This gave birth, as you know, to a world of pain, violence, wars, ignorance, karmic indebtedness and all the misery humanity has suffered ever since.

You all long to live in a world of Love and Light; but it is important for you to be aware that in the realms of Love and Light there are structures and strict rules that everyone must follow explicitly in order to maintain harmony, beauty and perfection. This is the only way that the "paradise-like" state you call heaven can exist. Heaven is not a place to go to, dear ones, it is a state of consciousness that you can embrace and create for yourself at any time, even in your dimension. When you develop it, you can easily create for yourself, no matter what is taking place around you, a true state of heaven on earth in which you can experience life as gracious, loving, abundant, and without limitation. This is LAW! This is TRUE LOVE! In fact, they are the same.

If you wish to ascend and live in a dimension of love and light, you must know and fully understand the LAWS that govern that dimension and keep it in such a state of great beauty and perfection. You must become these laws incarnate! I suggest that you start practicing now explicit obedience to your spiritual planetary hierarchy and their representatives, to your

"I AM Presence" and to the laws of harmlessness and love. When you attain that consciousness, I will meet you on the other side and you will know that the LAW has worked in your favor and not against you. It is my deep desire to champion your victory and your transformation. I offer you my love and assistance. Call on me whenever you need help.

Lord Maitreya, The Planetary Christ

My dearly beloved children, I LOVE YOU! Feel the sincerity and the depth of my love. I have followed the course of your evolution from the moment you landed in this solar system and later, on this planet, when you were still in that state of wholeness, functioning fully in the majesty and radiance of your I AM Presence. I have enfolded you in my love through the long dark night when you chose to create shadows and karma in which you now find yourselves. I shall follow you back into the realization of your own Christhood until you stand again triumphant, magnificent, FREE and Master over your human creation.

I admonish you to live for love through faith, using that love to expand the borders of God's kingdom, fulfilling the individual destiny of your own life, and making the universe to which you belong a sweeter, more magnificent and glorious place.

Dearest children of my heart, "blessed be" those of you whose heart has chosen an interest in becoming way-showers to the children of Earth. Blessed is the Light that glimmers through the folds of your individual soul, the motivating power which impels you forward, and which keeps your feet upon the pathway of Light.

In the Spiritual Hierarchy, I presently hold the office of the Planetary Christ. This office is held, beloved ones, for approximately 14,000 years by one Being; then another one who has qualified himself accepts the office. The preceding Planetary Christ moves on to greater service to promote God's will throughout the universe. During a 14,000-year cycle, the Planetary Christ has seven major opportunities to develop a spiritual education and religion within seven 2,000-year cycles, which will bless those evolving upon the planet.

The Planetary Christ works directly with the Maha Chohan of each cycle to develop a dual release of blessings, which stimulates the particular spiritual centers successively nourished by each one of the seven rays. Through these, the conscious mind of the people may be raised to cooperate with the spiritual movement of the current cosmic cycle.

You, who are to be the teachers of this age to represent Master Saint Germain as Shepherds of the race, must develop dexterity of thought, control of feeling, and an eloquent presentation of spiritual Law with their application. You must be able to stir the hearts and spiritual centers of the souls entrusted to you, for your teaching to have the transforming effect it is meant to produce.

I brought with me today the Elohim Cassiopeia, whose concentrated power of Illumination has the capacity to hold within the mind the divine design and pattern of Illumination. I also brought the mighty Archangel Jophiel, whose radiation of the feeling of Illumination stirs spiritual aspiration and encourages the up-liftment of the emotional body toward the Godhead. Through the dual activity of nourishing both the mental and feeling consciousness, you will understand more fully the particular qualities you need to develop in order to teach the people of Earth in the days and years to come. Allow yourself to bathe in the radiance of my love and in the peace of my feelings. I am Maitreya, the Christ in you.

The Planetary Spiritual Hierarchy and Beyond

The Order of the Masters of Wisdom, the Brotherhood of Shamballa, The Planetary Christ, the office of the Maha Chohan and the Seven Chohans of the Rays are the main body of Beings from the Realms of Light constituting the Spiritual Hierarchy for planet Earth. Actually, it is more complex than that, but my intention here is to give you a basic idea of who governs the workings of our planet. The different hierarchies for this or any planet could be described as a number of overlapping hierarchies functioning within hierarchies, all working together in love, harmony and oneness for the benefit of the collective.

Those filling these important roles are considered to be among the most highly evolved beings of the Great White Brotherhood Lodge for the Earth. The Spiritual Hierarchy of the Earth functions as a complex government and comprises many echelons. It is not within my domain to explain this in detail. To thoroughly cover this topic would be the subject of an entire book. Nevertheless, it is my desire to give the reader some idea of our spiritual government, who is in charge of various departments and what roles those beings carry out. These offices in the hierarchy are permanent ones, but those filling them change from time to time, as do the positions of president or prime minister in your human governments.

Helios and Vesta are The God-Parents of this Solar System.

Lord Sanat Kumara, the great Hierarch of Venus, has been the planetary Logo for Earth for around 2½ million years, perhaps longer. Until recently, he was here most of the time, but now has returned to his home on Venus, as he is also in charge of that planet. But he continues his work here for the Ascension of the planet and the completion of the dark cycle. It is my understanding that he will maintain his service to the Ascension of

Foreword

the Earth until 2012. Many beings have held positions in the hierarchy for a long time and will eventually be moving on to their next level. They are at this time actively training those who will replace them.

Since it is not well known who is replacing whom, I will give you the information as I know it. Although many changes are expected to take place after the Ascension of the planet, they will not take place immediately. The various offices in the Cosmic Hierarchy held by great Lords of Light at the present time are described below.

As these beings evolve, they move on to greater levels of service, being replaced by those who have attained the necessary level. Those who take on new offices are usually trained for several centuries to fill their new position. Changes in the hierarchy take place over a long period of time. The one moving on takes as much time as needed to train his replacement.

Lord Gautama Buddha is known to be the planetary Buddha, holding the title of "Lord of the World." In due time, he is the one who will be taking the place of Sanat Kumara as the Planetary Logo.

Lord Maitreya has held the office of the Planetary Christ for several thousand years. He is known for his great love and deep understanding of humanity. In his position in the Office of the Christ, he is greatly assisted by Lord Sananda. When applying for candidature for Ascension, your request is examined by Sanat Kumara, Lord Maitreya and Lord Sananda. All three must approve the candidate's readiness for the Ascension ceremony to be allowed to take place.

Lord Sananda *(also known as Jesus)* and **Master Kuthumi** hold the office of World Teachers of the planet.

The Seven Chohans of the Rays are headed by the Maha Chohan, which is another name for the representative of the Holy Spirit for the planet. It is comforting to know that the Holy Spirit is not just a Dove. He is a Being of great attainment who ensouls enough Light to radiate the comforting Love of the Holy Spirit for an entire planet, filling every man, woman, child and all life forms with his mantle of love on behalf of the Creator.

Maha Chohan: Head of the Seven Chohans of the Rays, representative of the Holy Spirit for Earth. This office is filled by Paul the Venetian who is also Chohan of the Third Ray.

- 1st **Ray** - Master El Morya
- 2nd **Ray** - Lord Lanto, assisted by Masters Kuthumi and Dwjal Khul
- 3rd **Ray** - Master Paul the Venetian, also the Maha Chohan
- 4th **Ray** - Lord Serapis Bey
- 5th **Ray** - Master Hilarion
- 6th **Ray** - Lady Nada with Lord Sananda, her twin flame
- 7th **Ray** - Master Saint Germain

All these departments have many sub-divisions. As you notice, some masters hold more than one position at this time. Keep in mind that each one of the rays represents one of the seven flames or seven God attributes of the Holy Spirit. There are also the five secret rays.

The Seven Members of the Karmic Board and the Lords of Karma: This noble group of beings plays an important part of the spiritual hierarchy. It seems that they have the last word in most major decisions. They are the ones who have the authority to distribute grants for the benefit of mankind or restrictions when civilizations abuse the privileges of their opportunities for evolution. Unless there have been recent changes not yet known to us, they are as follows:

Foreword

- Great Divine Director *(Sponsor of the Seventh Root Race)*
- Beloved Kuan Yin *(Goddess of Mercy)*
- Lady Nada *(Goddess of Love)*
- Pallas Athena *(Goddess of Truth, twin flame of the Maha Chohan)*
- Lady Portia *(Goddess of Justice, twin flame of Saint Germain)*
- Goddess of Liberty *(Sponsor of the Flame of Liberty for America; Her statue stands tall in the New York harbor)*
- Beloved Cyclopea *(Elohim of God, serving on the 5th Ray, also known as Vista)*

Chohans of the Rays

Channeled by Geraldine Innocenti – Bridge to Freedom
Excerpts from the teachings of the Chohans of the Rays

Maha Chohan: Few among mankind know of the great service rendered to humanity by the Lords of Karma. The name "Lords of Karma" generates much fear of punishment among those who do not understand the nature of their significant service to Life. Only lately has the love and gratitude of mankind risen towards this august group of Beings for their service of mercy rather than punishment.

El Morya: Divine justice, absolute exactitude in balancing the personal, planetary and universal use of life, is LAW! The Lords of Karma are instruments of that Law. The members of this Board serve to give to each soul an opportunity to grow spiritually, to develop and externalize the portion of the divine plan which can be expressed only through that particular lifestream.

Kuthumi: The Law of the Circle creating causes and reaping their ultimate effects is inexorable. Energy, magnetized and used, must return to the sender, as happiness, if the energy was used constructively, or unhappiness, if the energy was used in a harmful way. When a soul comes to a point of asking God for help for their actions of the past to set one's soul in divine order with the laws of love again, it is then that the Lords of Karma can give them much greater assistance.

Paul the Venetian: Because the karma created by an individual soul is sometimes very great, the Lords of Karma mercifully withhold the return of all one's karma in one lifetime. Thus the soul is allowed to mitigate as much karma in one incarnation as the Lords of Karma feel it can handle. This is true divine love, wherein much negative karma is consciously withheld from the individual until he has learned how to transmute it in happiness and peace.

Serapis Bey: When an individual desires to become a "candidate for Ascension" and asks for the opportunity to "clean his slate" of all negative karma, the Lords of Karma must be in one accord as to whether the aspirant has the necessary strength, fortitude, faith, illumination and general capacities to undertake to balancing the scales of justice in one lifetime. However, some individuals who have redeemed the negative karma they previously created through a long series of incarnations have only a small debt to the universe to "pay off" in the final incarnation.

Hilarion: It is the responsibility of the Lords of Karma to see that every individual receives as much assistance as possible in transmuting the negative karma created through misuse of free will. At the end of each Earth life, the soul is called before the Karmic Board and its experience is evaluated. Opportunities, potential services, seeming failures and successes are carefully examined. Then the Karmic Board sends the individual to a sphere of rest and learning where it can best prepare for another Earth incarnation, strengthened through purification, instruction and temporary respite from the pressures of its own karmic retribution.

Foreword

Saint Germain: Ponder well on the power of Mercy and the Violet Flame to dissolve the cause and core of distress and pain generated by the return of past misuse of free will. Then resolve to dissolve the effects before they appear in your life. You can consciously use the Violet Fire in action to do this by invoking it daily and hourly. This will assist you to transmute the negative energy embedded in all your various bodies and heal the emotions connected with those energies, embracing a new level of consciousness. The Ascended Masters' full gathered momentum of the effective use of the Violet Flame is available for any and all of you choosing to ask us to anchor it into your world at this time. As more and more individuals learn the efficacy of the power of transmutation through invoking the action of the Sacred Fire, we shall have on Earth a Brotherhood of Freedom who can, at will, free themselves and others from the shadow side of Life.

There are also the Seven Manus sponsoring each one of the Seven Root Races:

- The names of the Manus of the first three root races are not known. They completed their service to this planet and ascended millions of years ago.
- The Manu of the 4th Root Race is Lord Himalaya
- The Manu of the 5th Root Race is Lord Vaivasvata
- The Manu of the 6th Root Race is Lord Meru
- The Manu of the 7th Root Race is The Great Divine Director *(Saint Germain's mentor)*

All of the above work in cooperation with the Council of Twelve of the Galactic Federation headed by the Ashtar Command and Lord Melchior. The Galactic Federation council represents the spiritual hierarchy for this galaxy which is much larger than our solar system. They, in turn, work in collaboration with and are responsible to the Council of Twelve of the Universal

Federation. And it goes on and on, all the way back to the Supreme Creator.

At the Universal Level, Lord Melchizedeck, perceived as a "Father figure," is known as the Great Lord of this Universe. His great Light and Love embodies and radiates through this whole Universe. The Order of Melchizedek expands itself in several branches for each one of its many solar systems. People evolving on Earth can also apply to be admitted into this unique Holy Order; being accepted into this Order is an activity of the "Inner Planes." No one can be admitted into this Holy Order unless he/she is initiated by Melchizedek himself. It is not an activity of the "outer world."

Those who hold ceremonies and charge large fees to enroll their followers into this Order do not have a full understanding of its sacredness. In many cases only a ceremony is experienced and nothing more, not securing admission. Many dear souls may walk the Earth as full members of this Holy Order without any "outer" knowledge of their association. Others, who profess openly to be members, may or may not be. Admission is determined by the level of willingness for service to Life and Love and by the level of initiation of the aspirant.

You see, this Universe, as well as all of Creation, is well maintained by a long and indestructible chain of Love acting as the spiritual hierarchy, forever expanding to greater levels of Love and Light. None of them holds these positions because of a desire for power. In the higher realms, it is the degree of unconditional Love and selfless Service that determines the degree of attainment.

The self-serving systems of governments we currently have on Earth do not benefit the races and totally misrepresent the principles of divine laws and hierarchy. The form of government we have is outmoded and as humanity's consciousness evolves, will gradually be replaced with more enlightened concepts of divine government.

Only those who have attained the highest level of Light and Love will be allowed to govern after the Earth's Ascension in 2012. This will be among the requisites which qualify those who hold such sacred positions. This writing would not be complete without mentioning two more levels of the hierarchy. Their service is not limited to this planet because they are Universal Beings. Nevertheless, because of their great presence here, their service is important to mention.

The Seven Mighty Elohim and their Divine Counterparts:

- Elohim of the 1st Ray - Hercules and Amazonia
- Elohim of the 2nd Ray - Apollo and Lumina
- Elohim of the 3rd Ray - Heros and Amora
- Elohim of the 4th Ray - Purity and Astrea
- Elohim of the 5th Ray – Cyclopea *(Vista)* and Virginia
- Elohim of the 6th Ray - Peace *(Tranquility)* and Aloha
- Elohim of the 7th Ray - Arcturus and Victoria

The Elohim are builders of forms, representing the Father consciousness. They are part of the Godhead and are those who create universes, galaxies, solar systems, planets, etc. They sustain all of Creation with their Light which is of such magnitude that the human mind cannot comprehend it. They have created this planet Earth with their love and devotion to the Light. Their names are more like sounds and frequencies; nevertheless, in their great love for us, and as a courtesy, they have given us names by which we can relate to them on a more personal and individual basis. I am sure they are called by many other names in other places.

The Seven Mighty Archangels and their Divine Complements:

- 1st Ray Archangel Michael and Faith
- 2nd Ray Archangel Jophiel and Christine
- 3rd Ray Archangel Chamuel and Charity
- 4th Ray Archangel Gabriel and Hope
- 5th Ray Archangel Raphael and Mary *(Mother of Jesus)*
- 6th Ray Archangel Uriel and Aurora
- 7th Ray Archangel Zadkiel and Amethyst

These Mighty Archangels are the rulers of the twelve thrones of the Angelic Kingdom, which represent a different aspect of the Holy Spirit in the Cosmos. They are the ministering servants of God's Creation.

Last but not least, I want to mention our Beloved Mother Earth. She truly is our Mother who has supported our evolutionary pathway for millions of years. She is known by many as Mother Gaia, a name used mainly by surface dwellers at this time. This is not inaccurate, but nevertheless, on the Inner Planes, she has been known for millions of years as Beloved Virgo. Her Divine complement is Pelleur. She is a living and conscious being of great attainment and of exceptional Love and Patience. She has received much abuse from mankind and very little gratitude. **Let us honor and acknowledge Her today!**

She is considered by the spiritual hierarchy of this planet and Universe and beyond as One who is held in the highest respect and admiration for her courage and persistence. She has suffered on Her Body more wars, abuse and trauma than any being ever has. And still, she has chosen to hold back her own ascension in order to take with her as many of her children as possible. She has loved unconditionally all beings of her many kingdoms. She has provided a planet of unlimited beauty and perfection. It is we humans who have trashed her body and created ugliness here. It is our discordant thoughts and actions that are creating the harsh weather patterns we have to endure. When we return to living by the concepts of true Love and Brotherhood, we will have, once again, as in the times of old, perfect moderate weather all year round.

Through this writing, I have tried to answer questions often asked by many seekers. This chain of hierarchy goes all the way to the highest dimensions of the Godhead. It is much more vast than we know, and its gets rather more complicated as one goes along. We have this information only because the ascended masters have chosen to reveal this much to us. This information is a great blessing. We can use these names to call upon the beings of these hierarchies in our prayers and meditations for assistance and guidance, which they are always very willing to offer.

Inner Earth Hierarchies

All the hierarchies mentioned above also work closely and in total collaboration with the Inner Earth hierarchies, which are involved in assisting the Ascension of the planet and humanity. Who is in charge and how they function is not well known to surface dwellers. Let me mention a few.

The Agartha Network hierarchy is responsible for the inner earth governments of the various civilizations and Cities of Light.

The Masters of Wisdom of the Shamballa Brotherhood concern themselves with the evolution of surface dwellers. Beloved Sanat Kumara holds his seat of authority for this planet at his retreat in the city of Shamballa, an inner earth City of Light.

The Lemurian Council of Light of Telos is responsible for the city of Telos. The Telosians are very involved at this time in assisting the Earth and humanity in their Ascension process. They have been commissioned to teach us, when the time comes, to build our own cities of Light on the surface and to form our own God governments, modeled after the concepts of Light and Love which all enlightened civilizations throughout the universe follow. They are our mentors of the present and future who will teach us the principles of Christ consciousness in action and application. I am giving them the new title of **"Christ Consciousness Mentors,"** as they have embodied this fully in their daily lives.

In the past several thousand years, these names were not known, and people of Earth had no access to the tremendous assistance available by calling these wondrous Beings of Love to help and guide us on our journey back to Eternal Freedom through the process of Ascension. May you all be blessed by these names! Use them with a deep respect and gratitude. It will serve you well.

The Seven Sacred Flames

The Seven Sacred Flames

Master El Morya

Chapter One

The First Ray:

The Flame of the Will of God

Main God qualities and actions of the First Ray:
Omnipotence, protection, faith, the Will of God through the power of the Father.

Corresponding Chakra: Throat
Color: Blue
Corresponding Stones:
Lapis Lazuli, Sapphire, Peacock stones, Blue-lace Agate

Chohan of the First Ray:
Master El Morya
His Retreat: The Temple of Good Will, Darjeeling, India

Archangels of the First Ray with Divine Complement:
Michael and Faith
Their Retreat: The Temple of Faith, Banff & Lake Louise, Canada

Elohim of the First Ray with Divine Complement:
Hercules and Amazonia
Their Retreat: Half Dome, Sierra Nevada, CA, USA

About Master El Morya

Master El Morya is the great spiritual hierarch of the Brotherhood of the Diamond Heart. His activity of service and life is to guard and protect the spiritual focuses created as heart centers of world movements and religions, protecting whatever specific God ideas will benefit the human race and hasten its evolution. In addition, he is the chief of the Darjeeling Council of the Great White Brotherhood in India, Chohan of the First Ray and hierarch of the etheric Temple of Good Will. El Morya represents the divine attributes of the First Ray which are courage, faith, initiative, dependability, divine power, self-reliance and certainty. These are the qualities of the Father principle.

Embodiments of El Morya

- As Abraham (2100 BC), he was the first Hebrew patriarch and progenitor of the twelve tribes of Israel.

- As Melchior, he was one of the three wise men at the birth of Jesus.

- As King Arthur (5th century AD), he became the leader of the Mystery School at Camelot and guarded the inner teachings.

- As Thomas Beckett (1118-1170), he was the Lord Chancellor of England.

- As Sir Thomas Moore (1478-1535), he was known as the "man for all seasons."

The First Ray

Temple of Good Will

This First Ray temple is a magnificent white palace located in Darjeeling, India. From the steps of the palace, one looks out upon the grandeur of the majestic Himalaya Mountains and their ever-rising crests of snow-covered peaks.

The actual temple room is exquisite indeed! The altar, which holds the focus of the Sacred Fire of the First Ray, is composed of radiant blue sapphires and diamonds. The carpeting is an electric blue and the windows are of the finest stained glass. Those who enter the beautiful temple of El Morya gaze upon the royal blue flame on the diamond and sapphire altar. Kneeling before the Hierarch and touching the hem of his spiritual aura adds to the flame of the initiate's own cosmic momentum of loving, willing and joyous illumined obedience to God's Will. There is a great sense of warm welcome and graciousness which radiates forth from his focus. His beautiful home and temple situated in the hills outside the city of Darjeeling is dedicated, not only to God's Will, but also to the promotion of national and world government based on the highest principles of God-government.

The purpose of keeping this retreat open is primarily to magnetize, sustain and radiate the positive consciousness of God's Will into the atmosphere of the Earth and to counteract the negative acceptance of every distortion created by human mind. Therefore, it is of vital importance to have a certain number of unascended souls drawing the particular virtues of a specific flame into Earth's atmosphere and sustaining it through devotion, constancy and application of the Law.

Without the presence of individuals in your dimension who willingly offer their time and energies to magnetize, sustain and radiate the virtues of the Godhead in your sphere of vibration, there would be no stimulus to the divine spark within mankind to further its evolution constructively. Each disciple who "tunes in" to one of the seven rays becomes a radiating center of the particular virtue to which he consecrates himself, whether he is fully aware on a conscious level or not.

Thus, the disciple becomes the hands, feet and heart for the Spiritual Hierarchy to reach through the veil of human creation into the minds and hearts of men. Those who respond are accepted in a spiritual partnership between the Hierarchy and the masses who are not yet cognizant of the existence of the Ascended and Angelic Hosts, nor of the service these Great Beings contribute to their evolution.

Beloved El Morya, along with Master Kuthumi and many other masters, are determined to bring to the western world the knowledge of truly evolved consciousness through the Ascended Master's teachings.

Transmission from the Heart of the Beloved El Morya

From my home and retreat in Darjeeling, I bring to you the greetings of the Brotherhood of God's Will whose spiritual credo is "I Will." I also bring to you the attributes of my Diamond Heart which is rejoicing for this opportunity to share the multitude of diamonds my heart holds for those of you who are studying the limitless potentials of the Sacred Flames. The writing of this material has been planned by many of us of the spiritual hierarchy for almost a century, and it was part of Aurelia's contract with us before her incarnation to accomplish this task.

You know, dear ones, the time to remain in the consciousness that keeps you bound to the many challenges of your third dimension reality is soon coming to a close. And from all the complaining we hear from nearly all of you on our side of the veil, we know that most of you, if not all, have had enough of life as it is on the surface, and you are welcoming the changes. But consider that the changes you are hoping to experience for yourself will not happen automatically. You have to create them first in your consciousness before they can materialize in your world. Your personal life's experiences are always mirrors of your consciousness, no matter what is going on outside and around you.

You already know that the Earth has chosen Her Ascension, and life on this planet as you presently know it will soon change drastically. Have you made yourself ready in your consciousness and in your God mastery to embrace, welcome and adapt to all that is about to transpire on your planet? Are you ever so willing to detach yourself from the old outmoded and materialistic lifestyles that you are so accustomed to, to make room for all the positive changes that need to take place on the surface in order to usher in the New Golden Age of Enlightenment? Are you willing to transform your fears into Love in order to ride the wave of Ascension with the Earth in grace and dignity?

Are you ready to roll up your sleeves and pull yourselves out of your present complacency to take part in the creation of the new world? These are some of the questions you need to ask yourself and contemplate seriously in order to bring forth your mastery. You cannot become an ascended master simply by wishing it; you need to begin to practice thinking, talking, acting and feeling like an ascended being in order to attain the vibration that will allow you to become one. This is what we teach you in the Great Inner Temples and the Temples of the Flames when you come at night during your sleep time; and your souls remember it in your daily life.

Reflect on the priorities of your life at this moment. What interests or desires occupy your heart the most? Is becoming an ascended master through your Ascension your greatest desire and priority? Are you setting aside each day enough time to commune and unite with the seat of your divinity within your Sacred Heart to gain full understanding of how to become it? In a former transmission that you will find again in this book, Adama suggested that you cut all your "to do lists" in half and simplify your lives dramatically in order to consecrate more time to your spiritual advancement. Have you heeded his advice?

Are you choosing to create your ascension with the Earth or are you choosing to wait for the events to take place, simply hoping for the best? Besides your surrender to God's Will, the God qualities you need to develop in order to pass the initiations of the First Ray are courage, faith, initiative, dependability, constancy, self-reliance and self trust.

The sustaining of the Earth in this planetary system is due to the Love and Dedication of Sanat Kumara and the other Lords of the Flame from Venus. They have kept the flame burning on behalf of humanity for hundreds of thousands of years. Now it is time for all of you to take the "Torch" back, to take responsibility for yourself and for your planet, and return to Life a portion of what has been given you again and again for eons of time.

The First Ray has a unique position in this great evolutionary plan of Creation because this ray represents the "initial impulse" by which the ideas, born of the Heart and Mind of God, are given to Life.

In general, humans in the third dimension do not like change even if it is for the better because it entails disturbing the status quo, habits, patterns and traditions. The members of the

The First Ray

First Ray are fashioned in the purest fire from God's own Heart, and the crucible in which they are forged is fed by the Heart-flames of the greatest Beings who stand around the Sun itself. The day must come when the children of Earth welcome and embrace the plan of God for this plane and demonstrate reverence for it and for all life.

In order to be admitted into the fifth dimension, it is imperative that you express anew your unconditional obedience to the great Love, Wisdom and Power of the Celestial Hierarchies. In the higher dimensions, there is no democracy. The ones who have attained the greatest spiritual development are the ones who qualify to govern in a system of hierarchies (planetary, galactic and universal) all the way to the Creator Himself.

When an individual dedicates himself to becoming a "candidate for Ascension" or a "Teacher of the Law," and his motive is to spread the light with purity of heart and transparency, not simply to make a living, we immediately enfold such a one under our Wings of Love and offer protection and guidance. One must learn to become a disciple before becoming a master.

Believe in the gifts of your divinity! Let your Light shine! Develop self-luminosity, and let that light become the aura of this Earth until the Karmic Board itself may say: "It is enough." Already the Earth shines! Already her song joins the music of the spheres! Already her people have completed their curriculum of evolution"!

Time! Everyone wants time to do things. NOW! NOW! Let us do them this instant! Procrastination has caused the sinking of more continents, the destruction of more Golden Ages and the delay of more victories in the eternal tomorrow. The average person does not begin to set his soul in order until he is on the brink of the grave, procrastinating, satisfying the senses, putting off until tomorrow that which can be done today. Hear me well! If you can be self-luminous in a hundred years, YOU CAN ALSO BE SELF-LUMINOUS NOW!

I walked the way of Earth not too long ago. I knew the love of beauty and I also knew the trials of the flesh. Because I am called the preceptor of God's Will and the disciplinarian of souls, from which many men and women shrink in heart, there are those in your realm who think that I do not appreciate beauty. These ways of thinking by humans are so often very strange to us. Ah, beauty and order are heaven's first law!

In my home in Darjeeling there is, and shall remain always, both beauty and order. Disorder is not part of my nature, nor that of any particular Brotherhood. Disorder of person or surroundings is the externalization of human disorder in mind, feelings, etheric consciousness or just plain laziness.

In your own life, you will find that when you bring order and beauty into your world, you will progress more happily, for order and beauty brings grace and grace brings you the perception you never knew you had. Those perceptions externalized make you a person of "God in action" here on Earth. Now awake and come out of that soul sleep! Let enthusiasm spin again within all your various bodies; let those little electrons spin again around the atoms. I fire you with enthusiasm for the Love of God to bring this Earth back home with all its lovely spring flowers, with all its summer grace and with everything that lives on it.

I urge you to do whatever you can to assist the Ascension of our beloved Mother Earth and your own Ascension in the Light. Bring our Earth back home, bring the little four-footed creatures and all that lives back home for Saint Germain's sake, that this Earth may become Freedom's Holy Star.

The First Ray

The relationship between a Master and a disciple is a very close one. The Master accepts the consciousness of the disciple into His own sphere of influence, so that He can be aware of the activities, thoughts and feelings of the disciple. In other words, the disciple lives "in the House of His Lord," dining at His table and partaking of the hospitality of His household. This is an "invitation" beloveds of my Heart!

I am El Morya, your Friend of Light forever. And if welcome, my presence shall follow you each step until the hour of your final and glorious Victory in the Light, when we will welcome you, once again, among the immortals.

The Seven Sacred Flames

Throat Chakra

The First Ray

Prayer for First Ray Healing

God's Will Prayer

In the Name of God "I AM," I invoke the presence of Beloved Master El Morya, Archangel Michael and all Ascended Masters and angels of the Blue Flame Love of God's Will to guide and protect me daily and hourly.

Archangel Michael, come into my life. Help me overcome all density with your sword of blue flame. Cut me loose and set me free from all negativity and errors of the past.

I ask for a shaft of blue lightning of divine Love to be established over my being, over my home, my family, my work and all my affairs. I call the guidance I need to manifest God's Will in all aspects of my life to fulfill my divine purpose here on Earth. I claim for God's Will to manifest everywhere on Earth as it is in the Realms of Light and Freedom.

Discourse from Adama with Master El Morya

Adama speaks to us of the Blue Flame of the Will of God. He explains the spiritual benefits of surrender to the Divine Will and offers a wonderful meditation, which gives us a greater understanding of the word "surrender."

Aurelia

I feel inside myself a great excitement because I know that something big is in the making on the planet. I also know that the energy is shifting quite rapidly now and the veils of separation between dimensions are gradually thinning out. The ascended masters are in closer proximity and increasing personal contact with us, more so than any time before in thousands of years. If I compare how things used to be when I was a child, or in my twenties, to how they are now, there is quite a silver lining forming on the horizon. Even if the dark clouds are not yet completely dispelled, everyone is beginning to feel the changes. That is what I wish to share.

As we allow this unfoldment to take place, embracing all the steps, there is much magic in it. It took me a while to see and feel it, but now I really feel it, and I know. Those of us who are working, as teachers, directly with beings from the other side of the veil, are here to show the way to those seeking to create a better world than the one we have grown accustomed to. But ultimately, your life is your own journey and no matter how much assistance is offered, no one can assume your journey for you.

> **The next 5 to 6 years will be the most important and crucial years you have ever lived on this planet. They will determine what you will become and where you will go or be in your cosmic future.**

The First Ray

The planet and humanity have now reached the end of a major cosmic cycle. The Earth, along with those of humanity choosing it, is now moving into a new cycle of enlightened evolution. And you, as a soul evolving on Her body, are now faced with the most important choices you will ever make. It is now that you have to choose if you want to come along with the Earth into a brand new reality of love and light or stay behind for another long round of incarnations in the third dimension. It is up to you to decide if you want to experience the new world here or move on to another third dimensional planet in another universe, and continue to experience life the way it is here right now with all the limitations and challenges that third dimensional life offers.

The Earth really deserves Her glorious Ascension. The bells of her own graduation to a new cosmic cycle are now ringing. After all, she has shown infinite love and tolerance towards humanity, who has not shown in return much gratitude. She offered her body, so unconditionally, to allow us the opportunity to experiment with free will. The question to ask ourselves now is: Do I choose to come along to the next level or do I want to stay behind? What reality are you really choosing to create and embrace for yourself in the few short remaining years?

I constantly hear people mention they are so caught up in their day-to-day lives, that as much as they claim to want to do their spiritual and healing work for the benefit of their evolution, it is always put off for another time. They say, "Well, I'll do it tomorrow or next month, or perhaps next year when things change a little, or when my life slows down a little bit. Then I will have more time to do my healing and my spiritual work."

Do you realize that time waits for no one and we are now at that important threshold of change? What the Ascended Masters, Adama, Sananda, Maitreya, Archangel Michael, Saint Germain and all other masters are telling us is that the time is NOW. There is nothing, and I mean nothing, more important than your personal spiritual and healing work. Everything else is a distraction to keep you away from the "real goal" of your incarnation here.

The positive changes you are so longing for will only become a reality in your personal life as a result of that work. Bottom line, there is no other way around it. Nothing will change in your life unless you change it yourself; this is your job. This is what you came here to do in this life and if you don't want to do it, no one else can do it for you.

Yes, we do have to attend to the many obligations of our daily lives, but ultimately, what will really count and make the difference for you in the next few years is not so much what you have done, but what you have become!

Contemplate this. What we do comes and goes in the passage of time, but what we become, as divine beings, embracing our divinity from the perspective of a human experience, remains with us for eternity.

Hmmm.... Adama is here. He is patiently waiting for me to finish talking. Perhaps he is wondering who has been invited to speak here today, him or me. *(Laugh!)*

Adama

Greetings, my beloved friends! I am speaking to you this day from my elegant home in Telos, but I am also with all of you at the same time. We have with us today a silent partner in the person of the awesome presence of our dear friend El Morya. We both want to convey our deep love to all those connecting with our hearts through this sharing.

The First Ray

Today, I would like to talk about the Will of God as the path of "surrender." You see, without the Will of God you are not going very far on your path of evolution. This is the very first step, the initiation of the first temple that must be mastered before you can progress into the other steps on the path. If you are not willing to surrender to the "greater will" of your being, the Will of your own "Divine Source," how will you recognize your new home? If you are not willing to surrender to that which is seeking to bring you all the way back "home," the home of your divine perfection, joy, bliss and limitlessness, your lost paradise, then how do you expect to ever get there?

The Will of God is not a God outside of you. It is simply the God that you are and that you have always been, although when you are in a physical incarnation you tend to temporarily forget. Your divine Presence is totally omniscient, omnipresent and omnipotent, and can fulfill all of your desires instantly. You have temporarily forgotten that you are nothing less than an expression of this great I AM, incarnated in a human experience. You came here with an agenda to attain soul perfection and expand your own divinity to the fullness of your God-Mastery and Wisdom. You are here seeking advanced enlightenment and total spiritual freedom. You are here to become an unlimited God in all planes of existence.

This is an agenda of love for the Self, and that Self is no one but "you." Many of you are still so caught up in your mundane affairs, you are not seeking to attain the goals you have incarnated for. For too many of you, the affairs of your soul path and soul evolution have become the last concern on your agenda.

Well, my dear friends, when you are consciously putting aside the true goals of your incarnation for the sake of momentary human pursuits, your life turns out to reflect something very different than what you had envisioned for your life experience prior to your incarnation here. Once back on the other side of the veil, as you review the life you just left, there are always deep regrets. There is a profound desire to receive another opportunity for incarnation, to fulfill all of the soul's desires that you have denied in your present life.

And this is how the merry-go-round of endless cycles of incarnations for the soul keeps repeating itself again and again. Your divine presence, with great patience and compassion, has granted you thousands of opportunities. For so many of you, each time you come here, you ignore the reasons for your coming.

Lifetime after lifetime you did not meet the goals you set for your incarnation. This is also why you are still here facing so many challenges instead of enjoying the bliss of the light realms. You will keep coming back, again and again, until you finally surrender to the longings of your own soul. Your Divine Presence has watched you suffer, search and work endlessly for many lifetimes. It has observed your pain, your despair, your hopelessness, your fears, your tears, your doubts, your shames and terrors. It has witnessed the great wisdom that was gained in each of these incarnations, individually and for the whole of Creation. And it is longing now to bring you home, to freedom, to love, to mastery, to oneness, and to all that you are as a divine being.

It yearns to bring you back home, but it cannot force you. It requires your willingness, your intention and your cooperation. It requires that you embrace all parts of yourself that you abandoned and hated along the way of your many incarnations. Your GodSelf is calling you now to *"surrender"* to the path that is laid before you, day by day, with love and trust. Only through that loving surrender, step-by-step, you will be shown the way back to the "sun of your being," your divine perfection.

This is why surrender to the Will of your own divinity is such a divine grace to bestow upon yourself.

It is "you" who will be the great beneficiary of this grace. Someday you will wonder why you have waited so long to finally come "Home." Someday you will realize that you really never had to suffer; it was your choice. It was your resistance to the Love that you are that created all the pain and lessons that you have experienced for so long. It is now time to embrace a way of life that will nurture and embrace all of you, instead of one that diminishes you.

When you surrender, it is the human ego, also known as the altered ego, that gradually transforms back into the original consciousness of your divine nature. As you surrender to the process of cleansing and healing yourself with absolute trust, without judgment and without any fear, you can get through this rather quickly. The process reveals itself to be much less painful than it would be if you fight it all the way. The first step is always the hardest and most overwhelming part of the path. Trust that once you have taken that step, the rest is much easier.

When you resist what is best for your pathway, your soul will simply allow you to have your own way for a while, until you can't stand it anymore. Time is not of the essence for the soul, but we, the Masters of Light, know that all of you have suffered on this planet long enough. We invite you now to choose a more joyful destiny.

In Telos, it is with great interest that we watch the reactions of the thousands of people who read our information in the first three volume of the Telos book series. We have watched so many of you experience great heart openings. Your ancient memories have been awakened. We have watched the tears of hope and longings that nearly all of you have experienced when reading the material about our lives in Telos and Lemuria. You have become aware that a different type of life is not only possible on this planet, but in the making for those embracing transformation through self-love and spiritual wisdom.

With our assistance, this is what we are inviting you to do today. We have already trodden the pathway for ourselves, thus opening the way for you to follow into our footsteps; we hold our hands out to you, offering to assist you forward. Because we are here for you now, the way will be much easier for you than it was for us. For all those desiring to join with us and share the type of life we enjoy, the path of love and surrender is the key to your homecoming.

> **We have reached the level of divine grace we are experiencing today in our lives only because, a long time ago, we surrendered to that divine will. By doing so, our lives were gradually transformed, and yours will also.**

What we had to do, we did under circumstances that were much more difficult and painful than the situations you are presently experiencing. Let me say something about our passage to the Light 12,000 years ago. You might be surprised to know that after the destruction of our continent, we all had to work out our issues in the same manner as is required for you to do at this time.

Consider that overnight, we lost everything we ever owned, everything we had ever identified with in Lemuria and most painful of all, we were separated abruptly from nearly everyone we had ever loved. All the beauty of Lemuria, all our work of the ages, all the aspects of our day-to-day lives had suddenly vanished.

All that was left was "ourselves," the divine aspect of self that we had to surrender to in order to receive again "everything" from our Creator.

Telos was then in a primary stage of development, and certainly not the glorious and beautiful city it has now become. It was a large cave inside the mountain that we endeavored to restore as a city in order to save a small percentage of our people. After the cataclysm, Telos was all that was left of our culture. The city of Telos was still in a primitive state compared to the beauty and ease that existed on the surface, and to what it is at the present time.

Understand that overnight, we had to surrender our lives to a much different standard of living, which was quite difficult for a long time, having to forge a completely new life for ourselves. With great courage and determination, we continued to build our city not only for ourselves, but also as a point of contact for future generations, who will be born again here within the Lemurian culture. Having lost everything except ourselves, we worked very hard for centuries, healing the wounds of our losses and forging something new and more permanent. It would require several volumes to narrate all of the difficult challenges we had to face.

Our homecoming, a very long time ago, my dear friends, was not as simple as you might imagine. You are on "easy street" so to speak, compared to the obstacles we had to overcome. We ask you not to be dismayed by what you are going through in your lives; but rather to surrender to the process. Surrender with "willing acceptance" to the events that will take place on your planet. They will come for the purpose of your deliverance from the chains you have created. Simply open your heart to love and "trust" that your passage to the Light, as it was with us, will not manifest without your conscious and sustained effort. Be assured that the rewards will be magnificent for those who will endure to the end.

The Will of God is known as a First Ray activity, and it resonates with a blue vibration.

The Blue Ray is a beautiful peacock-to-royal-blue color. Its frequency is vibrant, alive and cleansing. It is connected with "the Diamond Heart." Like any diamond, the surrender to this Divine Will has many facets. Archangel Michael is a Blue Ray Angel and Master El Morya is a Blue Ray master, the guardian of the Diamond Heart of the Will of God.

The Blue Ray is the ray of divine power and leadership, the ray of power through the spoken and silent word, connected with the throat chakra. It is also the ray that is most misused by humanity. Each time you are not speaking words of love and compassion, you are misusing the energies of that ray. Each time you attempt to control or manipulate in order to have your own way, you are misusing the energies of the Blue Ray. Be aware, the misuse of this energy is often performed in very subtle ways—so subtle, in fact, that you are not even aware of it unless you begin to monitor from your heart all your words, actions, motives, etc.

You understand and know what I mean. It is the ray that will allow you to align to the consciousness you need to attain in order to be brought to the other masters. Master El Morya is known as a spiritual disciplinarian, and his discipline reflects the greatest love that his soul holds for all of you.

The rays are part of the basic curriculum that you have to master for this phase of your evolution. You have to master the God attributes of all of the seven rays equally, and now also the other five secret rays. There is not one that is more important, greater or lesser than the others. They need to be mastered, balanced and understood equally.

In different lifetimes, you may not always be working on the same ray. You are endeavoring to integrate and gain the wisdom of all the rays. You were originally created on one of the rays, and this ray remains your permanent ray. It is also called the monadic ray. But just because you may have been originally created as, for example, a blue ray soul or a yellow or green ray soul, it doesn't mean that you will be working on that one ray in every lifetime. In each lifetime, you usually strive to gain a greater mastery in two of the rays, and balance the others in oneness. You will do this until you have mastered and balanced all the rays at deeper and deeper levels, and until you have passed all required initiations for Ascension.

People come here on the Earth plane for the very purpose of forging their spiritual mastery.

Unless you diligently work at it, it simply does not happen. This is why you have chosen to incarnate so many times. You cannot expect to gain full mastery of the divine by simply wishing it or by association. It does not work this way. The perfection and refinement of the soul is accomplished through a series of incarnations in the third dimension. For those of you who live with the illusion that the space brothers are going to come to rescue you, hoping to escape doing your spiritual work to evolve your consciousness, you are setting yourself up for a big disappointment. Those thinking that you are simply going to be taken unconditionally into the light realm, I say, revise your thinking. The space brothers are not allowed to come and rescue you. And there is no need for rescue because you have created the lifetime that you are now living for the explicit purpose of soul growth.

The Seven Sacred Flames

In every lifetime, you incarnate back on earth because of a personal choice you make. You have never been forced to come back here.

In each and every lifetime, you choose the goals and experiences of your incarnation for the purpose of evolving your consciousness to gain greater mastery. When you are on the other side between incarnations, fully aware of all you left undone during your last incarnation, you truly want to return, to align and fulfill all the goals that were not met. You ask for another opportunity again and again, until you feel you have completed this phase of your evolution.

Each time you arrive here in the physical body, the veil of forgetfulness is activated; you feel trapped and cut off, totally immersed in the illusion again. Life on this planet has known many cycles of hardship for humanity because the consciousness of people living on the surface dropped to such a low level of separation from divine principles. Separation took place as far as it could go. The lessons learned, the experience gathered and the knowledge added to the whole has been amazing.

This situation is now gradually changing with the enormous and unprecedented assistance from the light realm, from the space brothers and from the civilizations of the earth's interior. Separation into the third dimension took place as an experiment to understand how souls would react once they would be totally cut off from God. All of you here in physical bodies have volunteered for this cosmic project; otherwise you would not be here.

This great experiment you so excitedly volunteered to participate in from the various worlds and universes you all come from had a beginning timeframe and an ending one, which happened millions of years ago. This grand experiment has assisted the people of Earth in becoming strong and courageous souls. And because of their great sacrifices, the souls of Earth are now being lifted into greater glory, forging for themselves a destiny so grand. You are destined to become the showcase of this universe and the teachers of the new civilizations to be born.

As you align yourselves with the Will of God through surrender, you are destined to become among the most "in-demand" souls everywhere in this and other universes. Planet Earth, which has experienced the greatest amount of darkness and pain, will soon be lifted to a state of great love and light, a way-shower for others to learn from. In truth, there is really no other place like Earth. Be proud and hopeful to be a citizen of this planet. You have suffered long enough; it is now time to come home. It is with wondrous anticipation that we are waiting to greet you and to hold you in our arms. We long to welcome you back to the valley of love, where the valley of tears has become the valley of joy.

As you peel off the many layers of hurt and trauma from the past, you will discover that you have a lack of trust in God and Spirit. And for you, "surrender" to divine will is a fearful proposal.

You feel that you have been betrayed and abandoned in this and in other lifetimes, and you enter into a state of fright. This is a core issue that has been part of the original fall in consciousness. The original separation from your Divine Source created pain. Pain then created the world that you now live in. Separation allowed for all the manifestations of individuation necessary to create the experiences you have had on this planet. How can you truly know God and your Self without experiencing the feeling of not knowing God? What first started as a little fear and doubt, eventually became a lack of trust in God and yourselves.

Your test now is to allow yourself to trust the Divine again and to reverse the consciousness that caused the separation from God for so long. The universe is a loving and a benevolent place, and will provide everything for you when you trust. "The fall" gradually took place when a few souls in incarnation began questioning if God was always going to continue providing for them. After several million years when your Creator always provided everything for everyone, without fail, many people allowed doubts to filter their consciousness and began contemplating what would happen if this suddenly stopped. They allowed themselves to fall into the consciousness that if God should stop providing, they would have to start providing for themselves. This distorted concept was at first held by only a few and eventually was communicated to the masses.

The fears that gave birth to this lack of trust then became more and more amplified until almost the whole human race completely gave up their divine birthright. The rest is history.

Surrender to God's Will presents to the soul the initiations, and the opportunity to restore this divine birthright. This is what you have to heal now, that lack of trust. To do so takes courage and commitment. Stepping off that dock of what is known into the deep still waters of the unknown is the ultimate act of trust. Let your heart listen to the call of your soul and you will know the choice that you can make now. You will know your true purpose here on earth at this time of acceleration and evolution.

When you chose to "not trust," God allowed you the experience and all the many consequences that came with this choice, so that you could learn the wisdom from it.

The fear that people have of trusting God is making the commitment to your Higher Self that you want to return home, to make your ascension and to gain your mastery. This requires

The First Ray

that you clear all the issues of your human creation. In the process, your Higher Self brings into your experience all the shadow material you have created throughout the ages. These issues must be looked at in order to give you the opportunity to make new choices in love and trust rather than fear.

All issues needing to be aligned and understood and any residual karma needing to be cleared are brought to your experience. The facing of all this can be temporarily challenging. You may think, "I made a commitment to start trusting God and my life has become more challenging." And then you choose again to fall back into the cycle of distrust. The path is to allow whatever will be presented to you, and to witness it, even if it is difficult for a while. No matter what the appearances are in your life, even if your life becomes temporarily more difficult, trust that you are on a new road and that the energy will finally shift. Compared to the millions of years of mistrust you have expressed towards your Creator, this homecoming to your true self can manifest rather quickly.

Think of Job in your scriptures. He was severely tested, but he continued to trust. And when he was able to prove to God that he would continue to trust, in spite of everything he had lost, including his health, his wife and children, all was restored back to him, and much more. But first he had to journey through the dark night of the soul, and so will you!

Allow yourself the process of going through this dark night. Finally face all that you have hidden in the shadows for so long. Do it without any judgment or attachment, because it is in these shadows that you will recover all your gifts. You will remember the attributes of your divine birthright, and your full energies will be restored to you. You will once again trust your Creator, as your surrender in total love will become your rescue, and not your despair.

All of humanity is basically experiencing the same path of evolution. There is no need for shame or regret because, in truth, you all have the same issues. Your current experience may look different, and it is the same way for everyone. Lack of trust and separation from your Source have created this long journey of suffering. Now resurrect yourself fully through love and trust.

When you can finally say, "I will let go of my own misconceptions and fears and trust the process, no matter how painful it could get," you have taken that first, hardest step. When you finally face your heartbreak and anger, it is not quite as painful as you expected. The process, when allowed, will take you all the way back "home" and you will finally experience the end of all suffering and lack. You will understand the universe and your life with a new compassion and softness; the struggle that has ruled your life will abate.

> **Once you have conquered that fear, everything is open to you, and you can have everything without limitation.**

Nothing is withheld from you anymore. You will know with absolute certainty that the universe that you have feared for so long will provide everything you ever needed and everything you ever dreamed of. What you call the original sin, which I call the original breach of confidence with God, is basically the last thing you need to conquer.

That correlates with the Adam and Eve story, which was a metaphor describing the lack of trust in God, which led to separation.

Yes, Adam and Eve is just a story recorded with little understanding. Though the allegory in your scriptures may contain some levels of truth, it certainly did not happen that way. The story of Adam and Eve and the fall from grace by humanity is very complex indeed. Some day, all the true records will be made available to humanity and you will finally understand and learn much from it. That story is simply a poor representation of what happened and not an accurate one.

What is representative is that people stopped trusting in their Creator and went into fear. Aurelia has among her possessions a little book called *The Sons of God,* by Christine Mercer. This is the story of a woman who decided to trust God, no matter what happens to her. Her trust was put to the most extreme tests. Through the hardships of her testing, she made a determined and heartfelt decision to never, ever again complain about anything. She continued trusting, no matter how painful it became. Even though she made this deep commitment in "surrender," she was most severely tested. The happy ending of this true story is that in a very short time she balanced such a tremendous amount of karma that miracles upon miracles began to flow lavishly in her life. All she had lost was restored a hundred-fold.

During the testing period, she thanked God for every difficulty she was experiencing, knowing that this was going to lead her to something much bigger and much greater, and it certainly did! Christine was able to take her body into physical ascension a couple years later, at a time when no one else on the planet did. She accomplished this when the energies on the planet were not yet supporting such an activity as it is now.

This little book made a big impression on Aurelia at a time when she was going through difficult period herself. She read late into the night, from cover to cover, the book she found for $2.00 in a used bookstore several years ago. Aurelia's reaction was, " Hmmm...., I guess my situation, which is by no means as severe as hers, could possibly be improved by using the same principles she did." She reflected in her heart that her attitude towards her life situation was far from being as graceful and grateful as Christine's was, and became aware that she was harboring resentment.

She read the book twice and then decided to apply the principles in "an attitude of gratitude" as best she could. Aurelia's situation improved almost immediately, and within a few months, she was again happier than she had been in a long time. Her heart was free and her financial situation was restored.

Christine's book is worth its weight in gold for the way she describes how she went beyond all her fears. The way this woman conquered her fears is a great example for everyone to follow.

I would like to explain the purpose of being tested.

Understand that God doesn't directly test you for the sake of throwing curve balls simply to be malicious. The testing is an opportunity you have invited for the sake of clearing and balancing negativity you have created in the past. For the sake of accelerating your spiritual growth, you requested the testing in order to allow the healing to take place.

When you put yourself into a state of total trust, the universe responds, and starts providing immediately.

God does not really want to test you. God is love and His love is unconditional. When you open yourself to the surrender we are talking about, the universe will provide all the situations and opportunities needed to balance all of your issues and heal them forever. With great amazement, you will soon discover how quickly the universe responds to your requests when you are aligned with Divine Will.

The First Ray

I want to express one more thing before the meditation. The minute you make a true and consistent commitment to your God Presence to totally surrender yourself to the process of change and transformation, your Presence will guide you the fastest and the smoothest way possible to obtain the object of your desires, opening of the "Door of Everything."

The Will of God is the very attribute that will take you all the way home through grace. Souls on this planet have to realize that before they can be taken to specific masters for initiations and advancement, they have to first pass the tests of El Morya, which are tests of surrender to the Divine Will. When you decide to make a real commitment to your ascension and to your spiritual journey, if you are not willing to pass the tests of surrender, how can you pass the other tests? Other masters may not be able to work with you until you have understood the various aspects of the blue ray. And then, when you have made yourself ready for another master, you are elegantly escorted to that master with a "recommendation."

I have been looking forward to giving you this talk about surrender. This is what is most needed at the present time. Going beyond fear is the key. As more and more people let go of their fear, it will become easier for others to do so. If you want to know how you can assist the planet, the most important thing to do is to let go of your own fears, surrender with Love to what is, and let go of all judgments. The more you practice this and succeed, and encourage others to do the same, the greater will be the pathway you are creating for yourself and for the rest of humanity. You can best serve your planet by clearing yourself first.

Meditation

Journey to the Will of God Temple in Telos
With Adama and Master El Morya

We have in Telos a temple consecrated to the Will of God. There is also such a temple in Darjeeling, India near Tibet. The retreat of the Will of God is under the guardianship of the master El Morya, both in Darjeeling and Mount Shasta. Many of you go there at night, or come here to Telos, to learn the initiations of the First Ray, of surrender to the Divine Will. They both exist in the fifth dimension frequency, and thus are not visible to your outer eyes. Today, I would like to take you in consciousness to our Will of God Temple in Telos.

Consciously ask your Divine Presence or your higher self to take you on a journey with us to Telos. See yourself arriving here in your personal merkaba, accompanied by one of your guides. Notice a fairly large opalescent blue structure, quite tall, in the form of a six-sided pyramid. As you approach, everything around you resonates with the beautiful blue energy, so refreshing and soothing. Allow yourself to walk up the mother-of-pearl stairway to the main entrance of the temple. Observe and feel the majestic blue mist emanating from various high fountains all around it. Many types of blue flowers, growing in white and gold boxes, are flourishing in great abundance and variety around the fountains, including the sweet forget-me-nots. Walk now through the entrance, where three blue flame angels are awaiting to escort and welcome you in.

As you enter into the large hallway, see a transparent chamber in the center containing a huge blue flame diamond, the biggest diamond that you will ever see, about 15 to 18 feet in height. Your guide invites you to enter that sacred chamber.

The First Ray

The diamond contains several thousand facets, each one representing a different aspect of the Diamond Heart of the Divine Will. This diamond is not so different from the one living within your heart, and in time, all the wondrous facets of your own diamond heart will become completely activated and restored. Your Diamond Heart and your sacred heart are one and the same; they are components of each other. They are made of an infinite number of chambers, each one corresponding to a facet of your own diamond.

Come into the sacred chamber of the Divine Will to be greeted, by master El Morya, a tall being with brown eyes who looks very much like a Zen master. He is wearing a blue robe partially covered with a luminescent white cape, with a bluish white and gold turban on his head. He greets and welcomes you to His diamond heart, and invites you to find a seat on one of the "blue-flame" cushions. He now guides you to focus on the energy of that diamond heart and to breathe in the energies, so that you can bring as much of this energy as possible back with you when you return to your physical body. This blue ray is the one that gives the power to the Love ray. All of the rays contain love plus the specific attributes of each ray.

In the presence of that diamond, you can open all of the little facets of your own diamond heart that are full of fears, and let them go. Intend for the energies of this huge diamond to magnetize and absorb your fears, dear ones, and for them to be released and healed. As you release these fears from your heart, you will receive a tremendous healing.

Be aware that it may be difficult to release all your fears and burdens in one visit. This is why we are inviting you to return to this temple in Telos or in Darjeeling as often as you wish to receive deeper levels of healing. Inner healing is an ongoing process until you reach completion. Consider your efforts as a work in progress, and be willing to stay with the process until all the veils are lifted. It is then that you will know that you are complete.

Now connect with your higher self that is standing right above you. Your great I AM Presence, the unlimited being that is really who you are, is waiting for all your fears to be released and healed. Connect with this Divine Presence, and make your commitment to surrender all the fears that kept you in so much pain so that you can be restored to wholeness.

No matter what may show up in your life tomorrow, it is only a mirror of a fear or old pattern of belief that you still hold within yourself that needs to be resolved and embraced. You will soon come to know, as you do this work, that there is nothing to fear except the illusion of fear itself.

Keep breathing this wonderful blue flame, as much as you can, directly into your lungs and into your heart. Do this consciously because you want to bring this energy back into your physical body. Also know that all the multi-dimensional aspects of yourself and all the beings of the light realms are supporting your journey home to divine grace. You are not alone in your journey; you have so much love available to you and so much support. Be confident that you can do it if you choose it. Feel the soothing action of the Blue Flame. It has its own way of bringing you comfort and lessening all your pains.

Now Master El Morya and myself have a gift for each one of you sitting in front of the diamond in our temple. We are going to superimpose a smaller etheric diamond of total perfection, radiating the qualities of the blue-essence, within the sacred chamber of your heart, right within the energies of your own sacred heart.

The First Ray

This diamond reflects your divine perfection. With this gift, the perfection of the Diamond Heart will be reflected to you as long as you choose to work with it. We invite you to start breathing in its energies every day in your meditation, working with those energies every way that seems appropriate for you. In your meditation, ask your higher self to show you which facets of the diamond are still holding pain or unbalanced attitudes that need to be healed and aligned. The diamond you have just received will continue to reflect everything you need for the complete opening and healing of your heart. It will take you to the path of surrender with joy and grace. It is alive and vibrant. Its color reflects a luminescent peacock blue.

Keep breathing its energies with allowance and surrender to what is. Be resolute in walking this path, and feel free to communicate with your guide. Stay with this energy for a while and be thankful for the grace you have just received. *(Pause)*

When you feel complete, return to your body, taking this treasure with you. The more you remain conscious and work with the diamond heart, the more its energies will amplify and bless your life. This is a gift or tool we are giving you, but it will not help you unless you use it. This diamond heart also has a vibration of self-confidence. Tap into this self-confidence energy to assist you to release your fears, so that your surrender can be accomplished gracefully.

The blue ray masters are available to you at this time, offering their assistance. When you feel ready, open your eyes. We invite you to return to this healing place often, to meditate with us on the Will of God, and to continue to make gigantic strides towards your spiritual freedom. And so be it, Beloved I AM.

Lord Lanto

Chapter Two

The Second Ray:

The Flame of Illumination and Wisdom

Main God qualities and actions of the Second Ray:
Illumination, wisdom, omniscience, understanding through love, perception, comprehension, precipitation, discrimination and activation of the Mind of God.

Corresponding Chakra: Crown
Color: Yellow
Corresponding Stones: Tiger's Eye, Golden Topaz

Chohan of the Second Ray:
Lord Lanto, Teacher of Ancient Wisdom
His Retreat: The Great Hall of Illumination, Grand Teton Mountain Range, Wyoming, USA.
Other Masters serving on the Second Ray: Gautama Buddha, Lord Maitreya, Sananda/Jesus, Master Kuthumi, Confucius.

Archangels of the Second Ray with Divine Complement:
Jophiel and Christine
Their Retreats: South of the Great Wall, China, and the Temple of Illumination;
God/Goddess Meru: Island of the Sun, Lake Titicaca, Bolivia

Elohim of the Second Ray with Divine Complement:
Apollo and Lumina
Their Retreat: Saxony, Germany

About Lord Lanto, Teacher of Ancient Wisdom

Lord Lanto, great light of ancient China, now serves as the Chohan of the Second Ray at the Royal Teton Retreat in the Grand Teton Mountain Range, Wyoming, USA. His devotion to the Flame of Wisdom and the Flame of Knowledge has truly qualified him to directly assist with the evolution of Earth through the Second Ray of Illumination.

Lord Lanto chose to use the Second Ray to embrace the hearts of mankind. He is dedicated to assist the evolution of this planet through the Cosmic Christ illumination. The Golden Flame that beats his heart is charged with the momentum of God-Victory. Lord Lanto volunteered with Sanat Kumara to come to Earth long ago for the rescue of the planet and her evolution at a time when total darkness filled the land. He was a high priest in the Temple of the Divine Mother on the continent of Lemuria.

In the last days of Lemuria, those that tended the Flames upon the altars of the Temples were warned of the coming cataclysm. Those responsible for the Flames removed and carried them elsewhere to places of safety, depositing them in other physical retreats or transferring them to the etheric octave. It was Lord Lanto who carried the Flame of Precipitation and deposited it in the area of the Grand Teton mountain range in North America. The Flame of Precipitation has a Chinese green tone with the yellow of the Second Ray. This flame is still burning today at the Royal Teton Retreat. Precipitation is the Flame of Abundance and Wealth, as well as Happiness, Joy and Universal Christ consciousness.

The Second Ray

Embodiments of Lord Lanto

- Lord Lanto embodied in ancient China as the Duke of Chou, also known as the Yellow Emperor, (12th century BC). The Duke of Chou is regarded as a statesman in Chinese history and is considered the architect of the Chou Dynasty and the true founder of the Confucian tradition.

- Lanto was later embodied as a ruler of China at the time of Confucius and held the Golden Flame of Illumination on behalf of the Chinese people for many centuries. Lord Lanto so adored the Trinity within his innermost being that the intense glow of that divine spark could actually be seen through his flesh form, emanating as a soft glow from his chest. He maintained this in honor of Sanat Kumara until his Ascension around 500 BC.

- He gained his mastery while studying under Lord Himalaya, Manu of the Fourth Root Race, whose Retreat of the Blue Lotus is hidden in the mountains that bear his name. Following his Ascension, Lord Lanto accepted the office of presiding Master of the Council of the Royal Teton and of the retreat itself in order to bring to the Western world the Flame of science and technology, the culture of the Mother and reverence for Life which he and Confucius had sponsored in the Far East.

Royal Teton Retreat

This magnificent retreat is situated in the Grand Teton National Park in Wyoming, USA. The glorious natural cathedral, which spirals above the emerald green setting of plain and trees, draws the admiration of all who come to the area. The Teton Retreat is the most ancient focus of the Ascended Masters on planet Earth. It is also the focus of precipitation, expansion of the Light through the Ray of Illumination and manifestation in the world of form. Its activity commands the power of conscious precipitation.

For many ages, within the heart of the Grand Teton, an order of the Great White Brotherhood, under the direction of Lord Lanto, has dedicated its strength, consciousness and presence to evolving ways and means of helping the evolution of mankind—for greater perfection of mind, greater peace of soul, greater health of body and greater development of the dormant spirit of God within the heart of humanity.

Lord Lanto conducts nightly classes at the Royal Teton Retreat, helping those interested in developing their natural talents, gifts, powers and reasons for being. A master of sages and philosophers, Lanto teaches us the path of attainment through enlightenment, wisdom and dominion in the crown chakra. The Second Ray is also that of illumination, perception, comprehension and education. It is the ray of directing intelligence, discrimination, discretion and the direction in the use of one's life. Those who are or who have been the great teachers of mankind are frequently Second Ray initiates.

Many great patriots, educators, artists, architects, scientists, inventors or great religious teachers received their inspiration at these Councils and have returned to their physical bodies filled with inspiration and passion, weaving their experience into a blessing for humanity.

Throughout the 19th and 20th centuries, Lord Lanto stood faithfully behind the efforts of Master Saint Germain to liberate mankind through his Ascended Master teachings on the I AM Presence and the Violet Flame.

The Second Ray

Transmission from the Heart of the Beloved Lord Lanto

From the great Hall of Illumination of the Royal Teton Retreat in the Rocky Mountain Range of Wyoming, I greet you with the Love of my heart and the Wisdom Flame that I AM. Throughout the ages, I have indeed served that wondrous Golden Ray for so very long that I have embodied it fully and become it.

When you think of the Sacred Flames, beloved ones, perceive their wonders with a sense of equality. There is not one that is better or lesser than the other; although each one holds a different attribute of the qualities of God, they are all equally wondrous and effective. Some of their qualities overlap, creating an energy field of Oneness. The seven flames are also part of the Earth curriculum about which you need to gain mastery and balance in order to qualify for your Ascension. Everyone who has ever ascended was required to master the attributes of the seven flames.

In our teachings to humanity, we emphasize the seven flames, but in reality, there are many others. When you fulfill your Ascension, the twelve Sacred Flames and their corresponding chakras will be fully restored within you and you will be able to use them constructively with all of their numerous gifts in wondrous ways.

In the ascended state, as you continue to evolve your consciousness in the various levels of the fifth dimension, and later on, in the consciousness of still higher dimensions, you will discover many more flames and many more chakras will be added to your lifestream. In fact, it will never end; evolution continues on forever unto eternity. How many chakras do you think your Creator or Lord Melchizedek have?

Shortly before the destruction of the two major continents, Lemuria and Atlantis, most of the Sacred Flames were removed from the surface of the planet and taken inside the planet or to the etheric Temples of Light. With the removal of the flames, also came the deactivation of part of your DNA, the minimizing of the Threefold Flame of Life in the sacred chamber of your heart, and the temporary shutting down of the five Secret Rays with their corresponding chakras.

Because of the severe misuse of these rays and their chakras in the two continents mentioned above, it was decided by the universal and galactic Councils of Light that restrictions had to be imposed on humanity. From that time on, only seven chakras with their corresponding flames were left activated for the continuation of mankind's evolution.

Many of you heard of the five Secret Rays and wonder what they are. Not too much has been mentioned about these rays by us because, although they are important and their energy is gradually being restored on the surface. The mastery of the God attributes they represent is not fully required until you get very close to the day of your Ascension. We do not want to confuse you with too many flames because the mastery of the first seven flames represents a big endeavor. Once you have mastered the first seven flames, it becomes much easier to master the other five. Though they are unique in their own color, vibration and attributes, they are derivatives of the first seven.

The stipulations were that until humanity wakes-up again to embrace their divine potential and the principles of Christhood, and when the level of consciousness has reached enough spiritual maturity for mankind to be trusted once more with this sacred energy, the knowledge for the right use of these flames will be reintroduced to Earth again. With the Ascension of your Earth Mother, those who have reached the level of

The Second Ray

spiritual maturity to become candidates for Ascension will benefit, in their own timing, from the return of their gifts.

That is the mastery you will need to attain as you walk through the initiations of the seven inner temples *(see chapter 4—pages 97-101)*. Once you gain the momentum of Love, Wisdom and Power on all the flames and have fulfilled all the other requirements, you will be invited to take your place among the immortals with all the glory and attributes of a fully ascended master.

That day, beloved ones, will be the most wondrous day of your entire existence. For eons of times, you have incarnated here facing many challenges in most of your incarnations, always keeping the dream and goal to make it someday to the Ascension doorway. Now this opportunity is offered to each of you in this very incarnation! You never have to die again for most of you, unless you choose it. The time you have waited for, is now presenting itself to you! This is an invitation from us, the Chohans of the Rays and also an invitation from your Creator. We love you all so very dearly!

Know beloved ones, that if you choose it now full heartedly, and keep this commitment to yourself and your I AM Presence, you can end, in a few years, your long cycle of incarnations to join us as an immortal. Once ascended, you will be working with us face to face, learning from us all that we have learned since our Ascension. Contemplate this for a moment, what took us so long in the past to accomplish, you can reach the same in less than half the time it took us.

I now invite you to look at my picture and contemplate the bright flame of Love that is radiating from my heart. I was able to manifest this in my last incarnation, as a mortal like you are now in your present state. If I could do this then, you can surely do this also in this time of Earth Ascension.

From the Love Flame of your heart and the power of your love, you can learn to expand your love to the point of creating a similar accomplishment. And if you work at it, I will be at your side to assist you and to champion your Victory!

I am Lord Lanto, your teacher of Wisdom, lighting your way back home with the wonders of the Illumination Flame.

Message from Master Kuthumi
World Teacher, Second Ray Master

Blessings, Children of my Heart! The beautiful wisdom of Creation designed certain focuses to accomplish specific outcomes. For instances, nature creates beauty to inspire mankind to return to the greatness of their own divinity. Your body has eyes to see, ears to hear and feet to walk. Thus the various bodies of mankind were created, each one for a specific purpose. The mental body is designed to create the mould of perfection. The emotional body is meant to fill your form with life. Your physical body, with all its faculties, is meant to externalize the perfection of consciousness in the world of form.

One of the most powerful avenues by which thoughts and feelings become manifested things is through the right use of the throat chakra, the power center for the spoken word. The spoken or mentally-formed word becomes the final "step down transformer" by which the desired manifestation is lowered into the world of form. This is done through the right use of affirmations, fiats, decrees and various forms of prayer offered to your mighty I AM Presence directly from your heart in connection with your throat center.

Humanity has been very proficient in creating discord, pain and challenge for themselves by the wrong use of the throat

The Second Ray

center. I admonish you to begin noticing how you create misery for yourself by the wrong use of your power center and by the way you speak to yourself and others. Resolve today to speak only words of love and harmony. When you learn to speak like a master, you will be amazed how quickly the world around you transforms itself to bring you the love, peace, harmony and abundance you so long for. What you create through your throat center always comes back to you multiplied many times over, whether it is created in love or in discord.

Each time you express yourself through the spoken or written word, do it always with love, compassion and wisdom. It is important to always express your truth, and it is just as important to pause, to choose the right words for your communication. You can always convey to anyone what is right for you and what is not, and how you feel about situations. It is not what you say or express through writing that creates problems of discord and karma for yourself; it is always the way you say or write it.

When you are not sure how to express yourself without offending the person you want to communicate with, go into your heart, take a deep breath and say: I now choose to communicate from the love of my heart. I invoke the Rays of Illumination and Wisdom to imprint my consciousness with my perfect expression for this situation. You will be surprised to discover how eloquent you may become and how you can transform a difficult situation into a divine solution. This is the Law of Attraction in this and all universes.

The Seven Sacred Flames

Crown Chakra

Prayer for Second Ray Healing

Prayer for Illumination and Peace

Beloved I AM Presence, blaze forth now from the heart of beloved Alpha and Omega, from the heart of beloved Helios and Vesta, into our individual hearts and minds, glorious waves of golden Flame of Illumination and Peace. Flood us with the precious oils of universal Knowledge and Wisdom.

Come now and direct Thy precious Light Rays of Divine Illumination and Peace into every aspect of our lives. Flood the Earth and humanity with the golden Flame of Christ Illumination, Understanding and Peace from the Heart of God in the Great Central Sun.

Divine Flame of Illumination,
Bless my world today.
Golden Waves of Peace,
Bless my world in God's perfect way.
Flame of Light so wondrous to behold,
I AM thy Wisdom in all that I AM.
Golden Fountain of Illumination,
Infuse every part of my being with thy Golden Oil.
I AM, I AM, I AM Illumination blazing
through my heart, mind and soul!

(Repeat the full invocation 3 or 6 times)

Discourse from Adama with Lord Lanto

Greetings, my beloveds, this is Adama. I am here in your presence today with several beings that most of you already know, or at least have heard of. Among those present are our brother Ahnahmar and the guardian master of the Second Ray, Lord Lanto.

Aurelia - Hello, Adama, we would like to discuss with you the attributes and uses of the Illumination Ray to receive a greater understanding of it. It must be that you already read our mind since you brought Lord Lanto with you. We welcome all of you in our midst and in our hearts; we are honored to have your presence with us.

Adama - Thank you, my friends. It is also our pleasure and honor to be again sharing our love and wisdom with all of you, and later on to a greater number of people through our published books. At this crucial time of Earth's transition into higher consciousness and dimension, it is more important than ever for every soul incarnated here to understand what is going on energetically and physically on your planet of evolution.

Indeed, more than ever, you are all in need of more enlightenment to fully understand and remember your divine essence, to know what you are doing here on this planet and discover the purposes and goals you have set up for your experience here. It is time now for all of you to take advantage of the most wondrous window of opportunity for spiritual liberation through Ascension that is offered to you at this time. Because of the deep love your Creator has for each of you, and through the most awesome divine grace that is offered to you from His Heart, you can now be liberated from the choices of separation from God that you made a long time ago.

You have been evolving here for a long time in a consciousness of spiritual slumber, which has created much discomfort, unhappiness, pain and limitation. Through the self-imposed ignorance and separation you have chosen to experience, you have forgotten how to manifest your lives as Divine Beings. Many of you have had enough of this unnatural way of being, and have called forth the intervention of your Creator. Lifetime after lifetime your souls have been imprinted with erroneous belief systems about God and yourself, and you have followed the limiting teachings of religions, whose leaders had for their agenda to keep you in spiritual ignorance, control and submission. For most, the religions and dogmas you have been so attached to believe in and embody kept you boxed into an endless stream of erroneous concepts that have prevented you from experiencing yourself, in your many incarnations, through the eyes of your divinity.

We desire to talk of a level of spirituality that is pure in its essence. We have often said that true spirituality is a simple concept that could be summarized in a small booklet. It is so simple that people have completely forgotten how to "be" spiritual and to embody it. You always look for the most complicated concepts you can find. Through the ages, millions of books containing elaborate and confusing ideologies about God have been written on spirituality. And in fact, very few, if any, acknowledge the simple truths that pure spirituality offers. A great number of your spiritual books have been written by those whom we consider the spiritually blind, wishing to guide the others of humanity who are also spiritually blind. True spirituality is a state of being, a pure state of consciousness that brings you back to the consciousness of Love, Light, true Life and your divinity.

In general, spirituality cannot be gained by the many things you do or don't do, neither by the many rules imposed on you by your society, your religious organizations and your governments that you are so eager to conform to. It simply "IS." This is why all the rituals, practices and concepts with do's and don'ts that you accept or reject were meant to be, at best, only basic guidelines by well-meaning people. These guidelines could have assisted you if you used them within the right perspective, but they could never inject true spirituality within your soul. You alone can do this in communion with your Divine Essence.

The purpose of our discourses and writings is to bring forth a teaching that is simple for people to follow, a teaching that will assist to bring you back to the consciousness of the "God within" as the great architect of your lifestream. We wish you to rediscover, as we have, the joy and bliss of living your lives again according to your own unique pathway, totally connected with this divine essence that beats your heart. We wish you to remember at all times that this divine essence that is alive and active within each of you is the only true "Source" of all that you can be, all that you can know and require to manifest your daily lives as divine beings.

The river of life, of love, of limitless abundance and of every good and perfect gift you wish to enjoy and yearn to obtain lies within you, awaiting your recognition and your dedication in calling it forth. With this introduction, I am now going to talk about Illumination, one of the attributes of the God-Flame that can greatly assist you in your re-awakening.

Adama - The Ray of Illumination represents God-wisdom, true knowledge and enlightenment in all its various facets. It represents Christ consciousness illumination, understanding, perception and peace from the heart of God's omniscience. It is literally an unlimited extension of the Mind of God. Many of the souls incarnating on the Ray of Illumination by divine

The Second Ray

appointment become teachers of humanity. A great number of the Masters of Wisdom you are familiar with, who have incarnated in the past as great teachers for humanity, are beings whose main soul pathway is the Ray of Illumination. To name a few, you have the master Jesus/Sananda 2,000 years ago, Lord Maitreya, Lord Buddha, Lord Confucius, Djwal Khul, Lord Lanto, Master Kuthumi, and many others.

Masters of all the Rays have also incarnated from time to time to become teachers of humanity because humanity must learn to understand and master the initiations of all the rays in perfect balance in order to qualify for the Ascension. Everyone has been created on one of the twelve rays, and millions of beings exist on each one. Understand that there is not one ray better than another, like some of you would like to believe. All of the rays must be embodied, understood and integrated equally.

The Illumination Ray is connected with the crown chakra known as the thousand-petal lotus flame. As you invoke the Illumination Ray in your crown, the thousand petals of your crown chakra start the process of being illuminated again, by expanding more your potential of reconnection with the true Mind of God, which has been lying dormant within you for thousands of years. However, it never left you, and this is what you want to awaken now. All the pockets of darkness you have embedded there through ignorance are basically pockets of the sleeping consciousness that prevent you from experiencing the "Mind of God" in its pure form.

When you invoke the Illumination Ray in your crown chakra and in the totality of your consciousness, and set your intention to re-awaken all the attributes of your divinity, your higher self will use the energies you are invoking to gradually lighten and activate the dark pockets that have been lying dormant there for very long.

Aurelia - *Does the Illumination Ray have an essence or a color?*

Adama - The Illumination Ray is golden yellow like the sun, and quite brilliant. The "Temple of Illumination" situated at Lake Titicaca in South America is the main focus on this planet for this Ray. The guardians of this Ray are the God and Goddess Meru who have been holding the energies of Illumination for thousands of years in that most awesome etheric temple. In Telos, we also created a smaller version of this majestic Second Ray Temple, as we have done for the temples of various Rays.

In the time of Lemuria we had thousands of temples on our continent representing hundreds of attributes of the Creator, and we had temples for every aspect of our evolution. We had over a hundred temples dedicated to the various rays alone. My beloveds, understand that there are many rays you are not yet aware of. You know seven and about the five secret rays; and there are many more. It is not necessary that you be aware of all the rays at this time, but it is of utmost importance for those aspiring to make their Ascension in this incarnation to gain mastery on the first seven rays, and later on, the five secret rays.

Aurelia - *What initiations might one go through while working with the Illumination Ray?*

Adama - It will be the initiations of becoming aware of all the erroneous beliefs you have entertained about yourself, that have occupied your consciousness and kept you in so much pain and limitation. It is stepping out of ignorance and uniting with the Mind of God. As you integrate and infuse yourself with the Ray of Illumination, you can invoke the Mind of God to do its perfect work in your own mind to transform and evolve.

There is the human brain and there is the Mind of God, which are not exactly the same. The Mind of God represents a universal consciousness that knows everything and holds no limitation. The human brain is governed by the human ego and is imprinted with fears, limitations and erroneous beliefs about the self. It has been altered by the human ego with its fears, and the consciousness of separation. However, it has been a tool for your evolution, and it has served you well. Your human mind, as it evolves, is destined to ultimately unite with the Mind of God. Do not plan to get rid of it like some of you would like to do. It is yours and you must own it as an integral aspect of your beingness.

What you need to do is transform it by right knowledge, true wisdom and by surrender of all your old beliefs that no longer serve you and keep you in limitation and ignorance. If you do this inner work to create your transformation, your ego will also evolve to unite and to fuse with the Mind of God through the infusion action of Illumination. In the process of Ascension, all aspects of you, including your human and ego mind, will be uniting completely with the Mind of God and all attributes of your divinity. Consider it an ongoing process for eternity, as there will always be another level, and another one, to open to and to learn from. The process that you need to surrender to in order to open your mind, your heart and all aspects of you to your divinity cannot happen overnight. This is the journey you have created and planned for yourself before your incarnation in order to attain the goals you set for yourself for your evolutionary pathway.

Gradually, you will integrate the knowledge, the understanding and the wisdom you need into your consciousness. As you do this, at a certain point the veils will lift, and you will unite your mind with the fullness of the Mind of God. If you don't wish to do your homework and you chose to stay in your present state, maintaining your erroneous concepts and belief systems, it is your choice; no one will force you into it. Be also aware that you will have to live with the consequences of being held back in your evolution while others you know and love will be lifted up into the next level.

Your own evolution is your primary goal for your incarnation, and it requires your willingness and your efforts to engage in it fully. It simply doesn't happen automatically. It is really a desire of the soul, and it has to become the most profound desire and focus of your incarnation. This doesn't mean you cannot enjoy your third dimensional life. In fact, it is required that you love and enjoy your life to its fullest; it all needs to be integrated as one. Your transformation now at this time of Earth's transition requires your full commitment and participation.

Group - *How can we consciously evolve our human mind to unite with the Divine Mind?*

Adama - Every day, invoke the energies of Illumination to unite with your human brain. Strive to expand your consciousness any way you can, such as reading material that inspires you, meditating, communing with nature, etc. You do not want to just feed the mind information, but you want to nourish your heart and soul with all that is noble, beautiful and enlightening. Go into your heart and begin to unite your energies with the Divine within you.

In the process of Ascension, your transformed mind will unite with the Sacred Heart. But the heart will ascend first and you will experience divine union. All your chakras will become unified, and you will no longer feel separated from the rest of "you" and of the universe. They will remain as different foci, but all united at the same time. Also, many more chakras will be added on to you. You see how powerful that is. This is why an ascended master is an enlightened being. You don't have to wait for anyone's permission or nudging to start this process. Begin now if you want this Illumination to take place within you.

Group - If I were to call on the Illumination Ray during my sleep, what initiations and process would I be going through? Where would I be taken?

Adama - We suggest that you call the Illumination Ray during the waking time. In your sleep you know all of this. It is in the consciousness of your waking time that you need to integrate the wisdom you learn during your sleep time. Who you are on the other side of the veil, as the conscious self, is very well informed and has no problem.

Aurelia - When I go places in my sleep time, I know that it is not necessary at this time that I consciously remember where I have been and what I have learned. I feel that it is more important that the knowledge I gained during nighttime be integrated in my daily life.

Adama - Exactly. You are not meant yet to remember your nightly adventures, because they are so wondrous, that if you remembered, you would have no more interest to bring to completion your third dimensional experience, and it would set you back. Once you set up your intention with your guides and masters to do and learn certain things during your sleep time, they will take you to all kinds of wondrous places that will assist you to meet your goals, but you will not remember. For example, if you want to go to the Illumination Temple, they will take you there. There are more than one on the planet, and you can visit them all if you wish. In fact, you have already done that more than once.

We also have an Illumination Temple in our city. We have created a bridge of light between the temple in Telos, the one in South America and in the Royal Teton Retreat, main focus of

Lord Lanto. In our realm, they are not energetically separate; we all work together as one.

Group - *Do we come to work on only one Ray during a lifetime?*

Adama - Not exactly.... In one incarnation most of you work at least on two rays, a primary ray and a secondary ray in which you want to gain more attainment. In one lifetime you could be working on the Second or Third Ray, but you have had incarnations working on all the other rays as well. The ray that you are working on in this life is not necessarily indicative of your original Monadic Ray. When you ascend you usually return in service to your original Monadic Ray.

Aurelia - *How does the Illumination Ray balance our mental, emotional, physical, and soul bodies?*

Adama - The Illumination Ray alone does not balance all of your bodies. Its main purpose is to assist the attainment of true wisdom, knowledge, illumination and the integration of the Divine Mind. Each Ray has a different action, and they all complement each other equally. Your world right now is flooded with misinformation. This is why right information is so needed and discernment so important to develop, which is also a Second Ray attribute.

Group - *Adama, would Gandhi, Martin Luther King and John F. Kennedy be considered Second Ray beings?*

Adama - John F. Kennedy was a First Ray being, the Ray of Leadership and of the Will of God. Gandhi was a Third Ray being of Love and Compassion. Martin Luther King was also a First Ray being. Leadership is mostly a First Ray activity, but not exclusively. Not only beings on the First Ray take roles of leadership in your world. Beings on all the rays also bring their gifts in leadership roles from time to time in order for all of the rays to be demonstrated.

Group - *Can you explain the misuses of the Second Ray?*

Adama - Some of the misuses of the Second Ray would be to use knowledge in the wrong way or to entertain conscious ignorance, such as not wanting to see things as they are. Entertaining illusions about life and self is also a misuse of the Second Ray.

I am going to talk for a moment about the heart. The human mind and the brain are tools that you have in the third dimension that have been designed originally to always be at the service of the heart. Your heart is connected to the Divine Mind of God, and until you reach a state of union with Self, your mental or ego mind needs always to be consciously at the service of the heart. In time, it becomes a natural state of beingness.

When you are constantly working or acting through your human mind instead of your heart, and not connecting with the higher purposes of Life, that state of consciousness creates a misuse of the Second Ray, through spiritual ignorance, control and manipulation of the Ego mind. Some people have great human intelligence but have no spiritual wisdom. They often use that great intelligence in the service of the altered ego instead of seeking their Oneness with All That Is. Do you understand?

You can only change your own perspective on things and embrace the energies of love, peace and harmony for yourself first, and then when you own enough of it, you can radiate it to others around you, simply by being who you are. When everyone in the population starts accessing the Mind of God through the Heart, your governments also begin to change and mirror the new consciousness of the collective.

As you change, as the collective evolves its consciousness, so will your governments also change. This way, you begin to see that it is never about them, but about all of you together. Your governments always reflect the consciousness of the people they govern. As you evolve, you will have the wisdom to elect more enlightened beings as your leaders. They are your mirrors.

Aurelia - *What are the side effects of the misuse of the crown chakra and how would it show up in the physical body?*

Adama - You know, the crown chakra is the instrument and the seat of the Mind of God in the physical body, designed to reflect knowingness, wisdom and illumination. Those who are consciously misleading people, controlling and manipulating, using their human knowledge for their own benefit , in time, will face the harvest of their creation as karma. Some of the ways it may return can be as mental illness, such as Alzheimer, Parkinsons, loss of memory or mental dysfunction or disease. As you get older, you are meant to get wiser and embrace more and more of the Mind of God. The opposite is quite prevalent in your society as people get older. Many people in nursing homes or mental institutions have reached a state of mental deterioration to the point of not being able to relate to their own name anymore or recognize their loved ones. Let us do a meditation and go to the Illumination Temple on the etheric plane.

Meditation

Journey to the Illumination Temple

With Adama and Lord Lanto

Adama - We have an Illumination Temple in Telos which is a smaller replica of the main Temple of Illumination for the planet at Lake Titicaca in South America. The majestic South American

The Second Ray

temple is maintained under the leadership of the God and Goddess Meru, very highly evolved beings, custodians for the energies of that Ray for this planet. At this time, we are taking you to the one in Telos, which holds the same energy frequency.

I ask that you focus in your heart and set your intentions to come along on a journey with us to the Temple of Illumination in our underground city. Ask your guides and your Higher Self to guide you in consciousness to come with us We have a huge merkaba that will comfortably contain all of you, and we invite you to step in for the ride!

See yourself arriving in Telos at the gateway of this temple. From a distance you see an eight-sided golden yellow structure radiating like a sun. It emanates its Illumination energy rays for several hundred miles into the atmosphere of the surface of the planet, also connecting to the crystalline grid which distributes this energy everywhere on the globe almost instantly.

See yourself walking up the 24 steps to this gateway of Light. As you set your feet on the last step, some of our people from Telos, who are the gate-keepers, greet you. They invite you to step into a specific area of the foyer to be immersed in a shower of Golden Light Rays that will clear and prepare your energy fields to be received in the temple.

At this point, each of you is assigned a Lemurian guide that will be your escort and mentor for your experience beyond the gateway. It is then that you are greeted on the other side by a most splendid team of Second Ray masters, Lord Maitreya, Lord Buddha, the Lords Sananda, Lord Lanto, Confucius, Djwal Khul and Kuthumi, extending to you all the love of their hearts.

They bid you their most heartfelt welcome into a beautiful entryway, like a huge portal, where everything that you see radiates like a sun. There are no words in your language to describe what you see and experience. Use your imagination to create your experience more clearly. Imagination is a faculty of the Divine Mind, where all past and present experiences store their imprints that you can retrieve later on in your conscious state. Allow your heart and consciousness to bathe and be imprinted with all that you see and perceive with the eyes of the soul. See how everything here reflects the golden sun of the love of the Creator for that Ray.

Notice and breathe in the energies of the numerous fountains of golden liquid light that spring out from the center and along the walls of the great "Hall of Illumination." See the flowers of all colors, shimmering with tones of golden mist, anointing their heavenly scent everywhere you look.

Imagine also a wide variety of golden yellow flowers of different shades and sizes, growing together in a most stunning, harmonious and spectacular decor, creating a symphony of love, illumination and wisdom everywhere you look. Pay attention to the details of the floors, walls, ceilings and the beauty surrounding you.

As you walk towards the front of a huge temple room, a large vessel is erected where the Unfed Flame of Illumination is brilliantly burning. Also notice the Masters of Wisdom who stand around the Illumination Flame, see how by their constant outpouring of love and nurturing, they create and nurture an ever spiraling expansion of that unfed Flame of Light. Without the nurturing of the Flames of God by those dedicated to that service, these various Flames would become extinct. The only source of fuel for these Flames stems from the fires of love and dedication springing forth from the hearts of those who tend them. By their love and dedication, they keep these Flames alive and bright for the benefit of humanity and the planet.

The Second Ray

Keep breathing in deeply, beloved ones. This is a rare gift offered to you at this time. The doors of this temple are not always opened to un-ascended beings. You are here today by special dispensation. I encourage you to offer your deepest gratitude to Lord Maitreya and the other masters mentioned above who have volunteered to hold the energies for you here, so that you can be allowed entrance. For those reading this material and desiring to experience the same, if your desire is pure and sincere, you can receive the same dispensation.

Continue to pay attention to the guide that has been assigned to you. Much wisdom and understanding can be shared through this interaction. Now you are invited to sit in a golden crystal chair in front of the master Golden Flame. Feel the energy of the brilliant Flame penetrating every cell and particle of your etheric body. Continue breathing in this energy as much as you can as you focus on this wonderful bright Flame of Illumination. It is about 60 feet tall, nourished around the clock by the love of our people, the love of the ascended masters and angelic beings.

Focus on that Flame through the breath and connect in your heart with the Mind of God and the masters of Wisdom who nurture that Flame. Connect your heart with their hearts and ask them to imprint their love and dedication into your DNA and into all your chakras.

Bring in your altered ego there, as it is also divine and an integral part of you. It is not a part that you can get rid of, but the part of you that needs to be transformed back to original purpose. It is destined to transform unite with the divine in the Ascension process. This part too needs to be understood and nurtured by your own self-love. Take that separated aspect of you, your human mind, your altered ego, and simply saturate these aspects with the Illumination Flame.

Talk to these parts with great love and compassion like you would a child. Tell the human ego that it is divine and loved, and ask it to surrender to the great wisdom of the Flame of Illumination to receive its love. Do this to infuse your life with a greater integration of wisdom and inner knowingness.

When you experience challenges in making difficult decisions in your daily life, always bring in front of your inner eyes this beautiful golden Flame of Illumination and Wisdom. Ask to be infused with the greatest insight of whatever you need to know in the now moment, or for the choices you have to make. This is how you will come out of unawareness and spiritual slumber, and this is also how you are going to learn discernment.

This is how your thoughts will become one with the thoughts of God and will assist you to come out of limitation. All the Flames can assist you in their own way to restore your spirit of limitlessness so that you can, once again, walk the Earth like wise masters and sages.

Also ask for this energy and this knowledge to be integrated in your conscious mind. You may not remember all the details, but the knowledge will be imprinted in your soul; that is most important. You all have too many erroneous belief systems imprinted in your soul that keep you in pain and limitation. Ask that these be presented to the forefront of your awareness, then understood, cleansed and healed by the Illumination Flame. It is a gradual process requiring your intention and your full participation.

Keep merging more deeply with the Mind of God, which represents the intelligence of the heart. When you feel complete, stand up and walk around with your guide and ask questions for which you are seeking answers. This temple is vast with many facets, sections and chambers. Carry on, resting your soul and

The Second Ray

your heart in that beautiful energy which also represents the Sun of your Divinity. It is through the Mind of God, through the Illumination Flame, that all knowledge will be accessed and delivered to your conscious mind when you align with it fully. *(Pause)*

Now come back to consciousness and into your physical body. Intend to bring back with you as much as you can of your journey into the Temple of Illumination. You now have permission to return any time you want, as long as you remain in alignment with the love energies of the Second Ray.

There are a great number of Masters of Wisdom in the ascended state serving in the various Temples of Illumination. Many souls come at night for classes and private tutoring with the masters in one of the many areas of these temples. There are no fees for the classes, except for your willingness to love and to evolve your consciousness.

When you are ready, open your eyes. Be happy, grateful and harmonious with self and with others. I thank you, my friends, for coming with us today. We send you our love, our wisdom, our support and our discernment. Know that you can tap into the Mind of God any time you want. The more you do this consciously through the heart, the greater and wiser beings you will become, and the sooner you will meet face to face with all of us. And so be it.

Aurelia - Thank you Adama, you are so very precious! And also thank you on behalf of the group here.

Adama - I am your mirror, my dearest ones. You are all very precious as well.

The Seven Sacred Flames

Maha Chohan, Paul the Venetian

Chapter Three

The Third Ray:

The Flame of Cosmic Love

Main God qualities and actions of the Third Ray:
Unconditional Love, omnipresence, compassion, true brotherhood, charity, Love in action, the love of the Holy Spirit, also initiations of the Heart Chakra.

Corresponding Chakra: Heart
Color: Pink
Corresponding Stones: Rose Quartz, Ruby

Chohan of the Third Ray:
Paul the Venetian, this Master also holds the Office of the Maha Chohan which represents the Office of the "Holy Spirit" for this planet.
His Retreats: "Chateau de Liberté" situated in Southern France near Marseilles, and Temple of the Sun, New York City, USA. As the planetary Maha Chohan, he also has a retreat at Ceylon, called the Temple of Comfort.

Archangels of the Third Ray with Divine Complement:
Chamuel and Charity
Their Retreat: St. Louis, Missouri, USA

Elohim of the Third Ray with Divine Complement:
Heros and Amora
Their Retreat: Temple of Love, Lake Winnipeg, Canada

About Paul the Venetian, Chohan of the Ray of Love

Master Paul the Venetian, Chohan of the Third Ray, also holds the Office of the Maha Chohan, meaning the "Office of the Holy Spirit" for the Planet. He is devoted to the Ray of Love and Wisdom of the Heart, which encompasses both the Buddhic Wisdom Principles and the Christ Love Principles. His devotion is to beauty, the perfection of the soul through compassion, patience, understanding, self-discipline and the development of the intuitive and creative faculties of the heart through the alchemy of self-sacrifice, selflessness and surrender.

He works closely with Archangel Chamuel, using the pink Ray of Love to open our hearts through art, music and color. With the assistance of Master Hilarion, they ensure that new technology and science has creative and artistic input. He also works with sound healing to help restore harmony and transmit to us the Rainbow frequencies of Light. He sponsors all those who bring the teachings and culture of the Ascended Masters and the Great White Brotherhood to humanity.

He, along with Lord Maitreya, is the initiator of the Heart Chakra. Call upon Beloved Paul the Venetian to assist you in creating all that your heart desires.

Embodiments of Paul the Venetian

- On Atlantis, Paul served in the government as head of cultural affairs. Before the continent sank, he went to Peru to establish a focus of the Liberty Flame, which later enabled the Incas to produce a flourishing civilization.

- Later on, he embodied in Egypt as a master of esoteric architecture and worked with Master El Morya, the master mason, in constructing the pyramids.

- In his final embodiment as Paolo Veronese (1528-1588), the great Italian Renaissance painter, he became one of the greatest artists of the Venetian school. Born in 1528, he received little formal training in art before beginning his prolific career. His exceptional talents originated from the Fires of Love burning within his Sacred Heart.

- Paul the Venetian was the influence and inspiration behind the construction of the Statue of Liberty in France. The statue, among other things, represents the Flame of Liberty, the same flame that Paul the Venetian gifted to the Incas long ago. He ascended at the end of his last incarnation in 1588 at the "Chateau de Liberte" in Southern France.

The Chateau of Liberty, Retreat of Paul the Venetian

In southern France, on the banks of the Rhone River that flows through the green hills and valleys of the rich countryside, stands the "Chateau de Liberté," which is the home and retreat of the Master Paul the Venetian, Chohan of the Third Ray.

The natural beauty of the countryside emphasizes the grace of the buildings, framed in the loveliest of nature's settings. Exquisite marble columns, adorned with blooming roses, encircle the formal gardens. Entering the elegant and spacious hall, you will see beautiful paintings representing the Holy Trinity, denoting the Third Ray upon which the beloved Paul presently serves. The building itself is built in three stories. Behind the chateau there are magnificent gardens landscaped in three tiers.

The service of beloved Paul and the Brotherhood of the "Chateau de Liberte" is also threefold.

- First, the development within the hearts of evolving souls, true love for God, love for Self and love for all life.

- Second, the stirring within the hearts of humanity, a love for cooperation with Cosmic Beings, Ascended Masters, Angelic Hosts and those who are the messengers of God.

- Third, by a sincere and practical love, the activation of the potential gifts hidden within the hearts of mankind everywhere. This love, impersonally but definitely directed, draws forth from the hidden recesses of the soul the talents, gifts, powers, limitlessness and attributes of the "I AM Presence."

In the new Golden Age, in which we are about to enter, every nation will provide for, encourage, subsidize and develop this 'budding genius' in their people patterned after the "Chateau de Liberte." Then the many souls who come to Earth with great gifts and talents will not find a cold, unresponsive world that steals the precious life energies of such potential genius to "make a living" in the outer world.

Transmission from Paul the Venetian

Beloved brothers and sisters, I greet you in the name of Love. May the blessings of the Grace of the Holy Spirit ever find me welcome within your heart, within your feelings and within your very Self.

I ask that you make every possible effort to truly understand the true meaning of Love. In deep gratitude, I now bow before the immortal Threefold Flame of Life cradled within the sacredness of your hearts. The presence of that flame within your hearts signifies to all life everywhere that you are a divine being, that God and the "I AM Presence" are invested in you and have some activity to perform through you, for the expansion of perfection from the Heart of the Creator, as a gift and radiance to bless your fellowmen. Through the love, which I can direct into your own heart flame, I hope to encourage you to believe that the divine plan will come forth and manifest in your personal life and on this planet as you apply yourself to become "Love incarnate."

Love should not be qualified with sentimentality, which is erratic and unsettled. Pure divine love is changeless and constant. It is the one virtue of the Universal I AM Presence, into which all the other virtues blend. Love is the highest expression of the nature of God, and in time, will be the highest expression of man. Divine love, unlike human love, is not grasping, but giving. The substance of divine love is the power behind creation, as well as the sustenance of such creation.

Divine love is a natural activity of the expansion of God. As we go up the ladder of spiritual evolution, there is a constant expansion of light, virtues and gifts of God through every Divine Being who has been created. It has often been said: "All the world loves a lover," but "human love" is merely a shadow of divine love which is an expression of the Third Ray.

Divine Cosmic Love knows no barriers and sends forth its pink essence everywhere to enfold the whole planet. When you allow the consciousness of divine love to rule your life, you become a magnet for love, and most important, to radiate this love to all life around you.

One way to expand the consciousness of love within you is through the application of the attitude of gratitude. When you express your gratitude to God, to your "I AM Presence" and your Higher Mental Body *(also called your Holy Christ Self)*, to all aspects of the various body systems, to any part of life, you increase and expand your blessings. The law of creation, manifestation and multiplication is fueled and activated by the feeling and expression of gratitude.

As soon as you allow your mental and feeling world to slip outside the presence of your own love flame and divinity, you are apt to feel the impact of others who unwisely do the same. But if you live within that Flame of Love, you will not experience that which would throw you out of balance.

Beloveds, never underestimate the power of your heart flame. When you allow it to be ignited by the fires of your Love, it becomes the power which moves the body as well as mountains. It becomes the blessings that pour from your heart through the glorious voice of your Presence. It is the light that shines so brightly that shows the pathway for others to find love. It becomes the energy that fuels your power centers to create "miracles" of healing, precipitation, teleportation, rejuvenation and every good and perfect gift enjoyed by those of us in the Light Realm.

These gifts are yours to own by using the right application of the Laws of Love and Harmony. The difference between your consciousness and the consciousness of where we presently dwell is the degree of mastery in the "application" of the Laws of Love and all the attributes of God through the power of the Sacred Flames.

We learned the mastery of those laws through diligent application over a period of many lifetimes. In your case, with all the tools and assistance you are receiving at this time of Earth's Ascension, you can accomplish in a few years what took us many lifetimes to attain. In order to fully succeed, you must become passionate about your desire to become Love incarnate through the increase of that fire within your sacred heart. This

The Third Ray

Love has to become your primary goal, your constant motivation and main reason for being.

We can show you the way, we can repeat our admonitions again and again to nudge and encourage you, but we simply cannot do it for you. I can make suggestions and offer you instructions to assist you in recreating yourself, but it is up to you to create your mastery.

If you welcome me in your heart and ask me, I will direct daily into your consciousness the ideas, the beautiful thought forms from the mind and heart of the Creator that have never been externalized before and which will assist you in embracing and becoming the consciousness of Divine Love.

You read above that I brought the Flame of Liberty to the Incas just prior to the sinking of Atlantis. I was also instrumental in bringing that Flame of Liberty to France during my life as Paolo Veronese. Around the year 1880, from my retreat at the Chateau of Liberty in Southern France, I worked diligently with some of my disciples in France to construct the beautiful Statue of Liberty that was given to America by the people of France. Thus, the Flame of Liberty has been burning bright on American soil ever since.

It is unfortunate that so few Americans today recognize the full meaning behind this wondrous Statue, not cherishing and guarding their freedom the way they should. They are too trusting in the illusion of the "American Dream" and allow their leaders to steal from them the freedoms that their brave forefathers fought so diligently to safeguard.

Liberty is not simply the name of a grand statue on the shoreline of New York City in the United States.

The Goddess of Liberty, the being who ensouls that Flame of Freedom for the planet, is also the guardian of that flame. She has gained the status of "Cosmic Mother" of a high level. We, the Chohans of the Seven Rays, and all those dedicated to Freedom, work under her sponsorship.

Liberty is a "real being" that we honor deeply. She is also one of the members of the planetary Karmic Board. I have given the name of Liberty to my retreat in France in honor of that Cosmic Mother. May I suggest that you connect with Her heart.

Tips for Regaining Your Natural Beauty, Youthfulness and Immortality

Think before you speak, act and feel: If you take time to think before you speak, act and feel, it will enable the elements of your bodies to return to their original beauty, harmony and peace. As soon as the pressure of discord is consciously controlled, the divine blueprint of perfection begins to reestablish itself as your Higher Mental Body (or Holy Christ Self) returns the electrons to their natural orbits and frequencies. Those who come to a state of mastery and peace attain great beauty.

Old Age and Disintegration: The appearance of your physical body is determined by the amount of Light used within the four lower vehicles—the mental, emotional, etheric and physical bodies. The natural emanation of Light through those bodies forms the protecting wall of your auric field, known as the Tube of Light. When the electrons move more slowly in their particular organ and cells, they draw less light from the Higher Mental Body and the natural resistance of the individual grows weaker. This initiates what you call "aging."

When you, as an individual, and the rest of the human race learn to remain harmonious at all times and the energies released through your various bodies is always harmonious and joyful, there will be no such thing as old age or disease. This is how, in the very near future, you will start creating your immortality increment by increment.

Growing More Beautiful as you Grow Older: When you learn to raise your vibration to a high level of love and harmony, and are able to maintain this frequency, as a way of life, a state of great beauty and harmony will be expressed within your lifestream. The bodies of ascended masters, angelic hosts and other cosmic beings are ever growing finer and more beautiful, as the energy pouring through the electrons is ever charged with more light, love and balance.

How to Draw Light in your Body: You have been taught the importance of drawing from your Presence the Light that is the food of the inner bodies and the only means by which their vibratory action can be accelerated. This is done, beloved ones, through the magnetic law of attraction. Your attention on the object of your desires becomes a funnel for directing it. As soon as you put your full attention on something and pour love into it, you immediately begin to create and bring into your world the substance upon which you directed your attention.

In order to intensify or increase the vibratory action of your body systems, you have but to put your attention upon any Master or your own I AM Presence. While there, you will naturally charge that substance of Light as mechanically as the battery of the car is by the charger. Simply to lie flat on your bed and visualize that Light pouring through all your body systems for five minutes three times a day would greatly accelerate the vibratory action of all your vehicles. I am Paul the Venetian, your mentor of Love and the Lover of your soul!

The Seven Sacred Flames

Heart Chakra

The Third Ray

Prayer for Third Ray Healing

I Open My Cup to Thee

My Beloved victorious I AM Presence, Light of my soul!
My Beloved Holy Christ Self, Wisdom of my soul!
Beloved Father/Mother God from the Great Central Sun,
Beloved Masters of the Great White Brotherhood,
Seven Mighty Archangels and Seven Elohim of God,
Beloved Virgo, our dear Mother Earth.

I AM so willing to be filled with the Love of God,
I open my heart to Thee.
I AM so longing for Grace from the Heart of God,
I open my heart to Thee.
I AM so hoping to become Divine Love,
I open my heart to Thee.
I now pour forth my Love and Devotion to Thee,
Asking to be restored to my eternal Cosmic Freedom.
As I AM renewed in thy Embrace
I feel the Peace of thy eternal Love Flame!

(Repeat 3, 6 or 9 times)

Discourse from Adama with the Planetary Maha Chohan, Paul the Venetian

Adama - Greetings, Aurelia, this is Adama. It is my understanding that you and your friends would like to discuss the all-encompassing Flame of Love.

Aurelia - Yes Adama, it is my desire as well as those who are with me. There are already so many things that have been said and written about Love, but yet, it is not fully understood, even by the initiates. We, as humans on the surface, no matter how much we strive to apply the consciousness of love, still often fall into duality and judgment. Please talk to us about Love once more, so that our hearts can be filled with the delicious nectar of that vibration.

Adama - My beloved sisters and family, I love you all so very much. All of us in Telos are so grateful for those like you who wish to understand the mysteries of Love at a much deeper level. Do not get discouraged, your full understanding is evolving, and as you continue to strive to embody this wondrous energy, it continues to amplify within you. One day, not too far away, it will be our great pleasure to finally invite you back among us, in the land of Love and Light. Thank you so much for giving me this opportunity to talk about Love. Though I am a Blue Ray master, discussing the subject of Love remains one of my favorites.

First of all, let me give you some background. The Flame of Love is one of the Seven Flames of God acting on the planet for humanity. The color of Love extends in great varieties of frequencies, tones and colors, ranging from a very light pink to the deepest golden ruby light, in thousands of love-ray combinations. Love is the glue and the vibration that keeps all of God's creations functioning together in perfect order, harmony and majestic beauty. Love is the ultimate healer and regenerator.

The Third Ray

It is Master Paul the Venetian who now holds the office of the Third Ray of Love, having himself become the embodiment of the pure Flame of God's Love on the planet.

The Third Ray is connected to the heart chakra, magnifying the Love of the divine and human Self. Love's divine qualities are, among many others, omnipresence, compassion, mercy, charity and the desire to be God in action through the love of the Holy Spirit. Because of his mastery of the eternal Flame of Cosmic Love, Master Paul the Venetian also holds the office of the Maha Chohan for the planet. In this position in the hierarchy, he embodies at this time the energy of what is known to you as the Office of the Holy Spirit. This is a very complex and wondrous office that could fill many chapters of a book.

There are several retreats or temples of the Love Flame on the planet. We have a beautiful Temple of Love here in Telos, and there are Temples of Love in all the subterranean and etheric cities of Light, not only on this planet, but throughout this and other universes. Paul the Venetian, a Frenchman in his last incarnation, is the guardian of an etheric retreat of the Third Ray below the Chateau of Liberty in Southern France. He has another retreat beneath the Temple of the Sun in New York City. There is also a spiritual retreat of the Elohim of Love, Heros and Amora, twin flames of Love, around Lake Winnipeg, in Manitoba, Canada, and another awesome temple created and guarded by the Third Ray Archangels, twin flames of Love, Chamuel and Charity, in St. Louis, Missouri, USA.

Let me now speak of Love for a moment, as the only true and permanent force in all creation, and then I will invite Paul the Venetian to address you.

Love is not a word. It is an essence, a power and a vibration. It is Life! Love is the most priceless element and vibration in all existence, an eternal dynamic living force. It is the golden chariot that transcends time and eliminates space. Love is the primal substance of Light out of which all things are created. It is the unified power which holds all things together. Love simply contains everything. Enough intensity of love can heal and transform everything. Just as there is no real dividing barrier between your human self and your Grand Cosmic Self, there is no real dividing barrier between your human love and your Christ Love. There is only a difference in intensity and vibration. It is human love embodied and amplified a few million times.

There are those in incarnation who perceive love as a weakness. Love is certainly not a weakness, but the greatest strength. Love is the most important God-attribute that you can cultivate and develop. Its power can endure all things, rejoice in all things and glorify all things. Love is a constant force from which you can draw life's energies and harmony. Its healing tenderness penetrates all things and enfolds every heart. When one develops this great God-given faculty of Love, he will have the power to create and bring forth whatever his purified spiritual vision of love beholds.

For those who have perfected the fires of love, fear can no longer exist. Your higher Self has the ability to transform, instantly, huge amounts of human negativity into pure Love and Light. When the acquisition of this great gift of Love becomes the one main goal and desire in your life, when it has become a burning obsession that can no longer be denied, then it will be fulfilled. Such a one becomes the recipient of a Love so great that walls of glory are created around that individual, and nothing less than pure love can ever touch him again.

To those who attain this divine gift of Love, the realms of Light open wide, and all powers are again bestowed upon them. Beauty, youthfulness and vitality in all their divine perfection, power and abundance in majesty, the all knowingness of the Mind of God and all spiritual attributes restored in full measure are the gifts of perfected Love. Pray to God and your divine Presence with all the energy of your heart that you may open yourself to this divine Christ-like love. Let this love begin to sing as a song of adoration and gratitude in your heart. Let your heart be lifted up continually by your heart songs of everlasting joy and gratitude, and this great love will become yours. Wherever you are, all powers and treasures of the higher realms will be bestowed upon you in heaven and on Earth, forever unto eternity.

These treasures of heaven are the divine gifts and qualities a man develops as he releases the hidden, God-given potentials within Self, within the Sacred Heart, the seat of your divinity. These gifts and powers that God holds forth for all of you are His plan for your full restoration, as divine beings, as He waits patiently for you to fully accept them.

Within each of you is held your cosmic bank account into which your merits are deposited or withdrawn. In the next world, mankind is not evaluated by his possessions or his human learning, neither by earthly positions or honors. A man is seen by what he IS, the level of his spiritual attainment. What he has become as a divine being is the only measure of evaluating all he has thought, felt and done. This Christ Light garment of pure Love, apparel of effulgent power and beauty is brought forth from within as one begins to lay for himself his treasures in heaven. The glorified white raiment of Light that will be bestowed upon you is the outflowing interest that accrues from one's deposits made of love, compassion, mercy, tenderness, gratitude and praise.

As you apply yourself to embody that Christ-like Love, rejoice in these dynamic treasures of fulfillment as heaven yields its wealth and its unlimited interest in your cosmic bank account multiplied a hundred-fold! Yea, and so much more!

To give you some idea, most of the souls of humanity at the present time still have the Flame of Love burning in their heart at a level of 1/16th to 1/8th of an inch. Many of you through diligence and determination have reached a greater level, but you still have a ways to go. When the fires of Love within your heart burn a Flame nine feet tall, you will know that you have attained what it takes to finally be carried "home" on "Wings of Light" and be admitted among the immortals.

Aurelia - Wow, this sounds wonderful Adama! I want to attain this. Thanks for reminding us again. I have known about this wondrous Love, but I have not fully understood it. What is keeping us from exploding into the fullness of our divinity, from this burning desire to realize perfected love?

Adama - There are several factors, and I am going to mention a few. You can figure out the rest. Not all apply to you personally, but in general, several of these factors apply to most people in varying degrees. First, lack of vigilance and motivation, with too little faith in such promises. A lack of consistency in your resolution to invest enough time and energy in your spiritual development keeps you in a state of spiritual lethargy and in a spiritual negative balance. Your desires for love and ascension are still in a lukewarm stage.

Until it becomes a burning desire in your heart and soul, so great that you can no longer live without it, you cannot generate enough love, power and energy to attain this level of evolution.

I will say that most of you are suffering from a kind of spiritual laziness, keeping yourself too busy "doing" rather than "becoming." For many of you who have laid out your spiritual goals, you then find an excuse to avoid your commitment to them. Many of you have not yet taken the time to seriously sit with "yourself" to write out your spiritual goals for this incarnation. Have you seriously contemplated how you are going to reach those goals? How many of you possess a full understanding of why you have chosen to incarnate here at this time?

We suggest that you start now by slashing all your "to do lists" in half and invest yourself in developing and integrating the true love of your Divinity. This takes time, love of self, effort and commitment on an ongoing basis; it simply does not happen on its own.

Many of you have delegated your evolution "to chance" for too many lifetimes, and you are still here in pain and lack. In truth, there is nothing more important for you to be doing at this time. Remember, what you do today, tomorrow and what you did yesterday has a very short-term impact on your lives. But what you "become" as a divine being incarnated in a human experience remains with you for eternity. Which is more important?

You will say to me, "But Adama, we have to make a livelihood and take care of our third dimensional obligations." And I say to you, "Yes you do, and it is important for you to take care of your daily life with an impeccable spiritual perspective. It is within the context of daily life that you build your character and develop your God-hidden qualities."

If you prioritize your goals correctly and learn to manage your time appropriately, you will let go of your activities, social and otherwise, that from our perspective, are a waste of your time and energy. All of you would be able to find at least one hour a day and more to invest in your spiritual life, and in communion with your Divine Self. It is imperative that all of you start managing your time more effectively. It is part of the curriculum of becoming a Master of Wisdom. Be creative! How do you expect to unite in love and divinity with an aspect of your Godhood, if you have no real interest in investing the time to get acquainted with it?

You can start speaking less and pondering more the wonders and splendor of the God-within. Meditate or contemplate your inner divinity while taking your nature walks. Cut most of your television and chitchat time, as it does not serve your spiritual evolution. Most of you can spend less time in stores. Nearly all of you have become addicted to shopping for more things than you really need, that only add to the clutter of your homes. This will save money that you can use for more important endeavors. In the light realm, we are amazed and puzzled to see how addicted to shopping and touring the shopping centers, constantly searching for new gadgets to buy, this whole generation has become. You get the picture, don't you? There are quite a few more factors I could mention about your human habits that keep you glued to the third dimension, but I leave it up to you to discover the rest.

Take time to review your life and know why you are here and where you are going. Take time to create a spiritual plan for yourself, and I promise that you will never regret it.

There are three kinds of people: those who make things happen, those who watch what happens and those who have no idea what happened. If you want to ride on the ascension wagon in this lifetime, you have to join the category of people who make things happen. This means that you have to actively create and pursue all that is required for your lifestream to be admitted into the great Halls of Ascension in this exceptional window of opportunity for Ascension at this time. Otherwise, it will simply not happen for you in this cycle. It will not happen by association, but by your constant efforts and determination to create it.

You will also have to stick with the process of daily purification and transmutation until it literally happens. No matter what you have to go through at times to balance all your debts towards life, if the fire of your hearts is burning high enough, this love stands ready to see you through all potential tribulations with ease and grace.

Aurelia - *You are very clear and concise in your explanations.*

Adama - I am, because many of you are running out of time. You have been procrastinating far too long, and you now have less than five years left to embrace the journey to the great planetary Ascension party planned for the year 2012. Most of you underestimate the seriousness and the levels of commitment necessary to make a physical ascension on a conscious level. Of course, there will always be another opportunity at a later time, and 2012 is not the end, but a beginning of an Ascension cycle for the planet. Those who procrastinate now may not meet the requirements on time, and will certainly experience much regret.

Now I invite Paul the Venetian to speak to you

Paul the Venetian - Beloved children of my heart! I greet you in the Flame of Love. May the blessings of the grace of the Holy Spirit ever find me welcome within your heart, your feelings, and your very soul! Gentle as a pure white dove, which symbolizes His consciousness, the grace and humility of the Holy Spirit drawn out of the sweet delicate rhythm of its reverent song of being, are often overlooked by the Western mind. When a man comes to a place of "listening grace," when all of the restless energies of his many selves are stilled, then do the beauty, the grace, the benedictions and the presence of the Holy Spirit flow. As the wings of the dove carry her high, her freedom is manifest in "being," not so much in doing.

When one lives and serves according to the guidance of the Divine Self, there is happiness and fulfillment in that service. When one is developing new momentum, there are growing pains, and both are essential to mature consciousness.

When the lifestream of the disciple is earnest and sincere, he makes the effort to always be in the perfect place where the wisdom of the I AM Presence requires him to be. Life will then always cooperate and guide that lifestream where the greatest service and advancement can be rendered.

Our words are crystal cups that carry love and peace into the outer consciousness of those of mankind who have a remembrance of spiritual friendship and sweet association with us at inner levels. Through the magnetic power of the Three-fold Flame within the Heart, the attention of the masters of the higher realms can be drawn to you for greater assistance.

One of the main sources of unhappiness, frustration and distress experienced by mankind is the capacity and willingness to disobey the divine directions of their own individualized I AM Presence and the guidance of the Ascended Hosts of Light. There is always a choice between joyous, willing, illumined obedience to the directions of that Presence and the willful and ignorant misuse of the free will to create imperfection. It becomes a personal choice and matter between each man and his God.

Until each member of the human race comes to a personal desire to do the Will of God and live by the laws of Love, he will not experience permanent happiness or the joy of victorious accomplishment, which brings peace, abundance, limitless love and a spiritual expansion not yet known to your outer mind.

Man has not destroyed the conscious connection with his own individualized I AM Presence in a moment, nor can he establish anew such a connection in a moment. It requires patience, persistence, determination, purity of motives, a well-developed sense of discrimination and a constant vigilance at the door of the heart of the Presence.

The Presence of God is waiting, waiting for the opportunity to serve through you. The beautiful, loving, all-powerful Father of Life stands in a constant attitude of listening. Whenever He is called, He answers with an onrush of His mighty Presence through the instruments created and prepared by His love.

Beloved children of the Father/Mother of Life, could your eyes but see the imminence of the Holy Presence when your innocent forms rise from their beds and place their feet upon the pathway of the day, you would understand the rudeness of the outer self in keeping the Presence waiting. In the midst of unimportant things, sometimes a day, a week or a lifetime passes, and the Presence of God is still waiting for the opportunity to fill your cup with grace, peace, abundance, healing and love.

And so, my beloved children, proceeding through the veil of human experience, remember, when your feet step upon the ground each morning that the Presence of God is waiting to fill your day with the fullness of your divinity, if you choose to invite it! Remember today, as you read these lines, the Presence of God is waiting to bless each of you with the fullness of the Love and Peace beyond all understanding. Invoke that Presence each day and each hour of the day to be filled with that Love, Peace and Harmony that will grace your lives to experience ease and perfection.

Codes of Conduct for a Disciple of the Holy Spirit

The Maha Chohan

1. Become conscious always of your aspiration to embody the full expression of Godhood, and devote all of your being and service to that end.

2. Learn the lessons of harmlessness—neither by word, nor thought, nor feeling will you ever inflict evil or harm upon any part of life. Know that action and physical violence will keep you in the realm of pain, suffering and mortality.

3. Stir not a brother's sea of emotion thoughtlessly or deliberately. Know that the storm in which you would place his spirit will sooner or later flow upon the banks of your own lifestream. Rather bring always tranquility, love, harmony and peace to all life.

4. Disassociate yourself from the personal and planetary delusion. Never allow yourself to love your little self more than the harmony of the universe. If you are right, there is no need to acclaim it. If you are wrong, pray for forgiveness.

5. Walk gently upon the Earth and through the universe, knowing that the body is a sacred temple, in which dwells the Holy Spirit, bringing peace and illumination to life everywhere. Keep your temple always in a respectful and purified manner, as befitting the habitation of the Spirit of Love and Truth. Respect and honor with gentle dignity all other temples, knowing that often within a crude exterior burns a great light.

6. In the presence of Nature, absorb the beauties and gifts of Her kingdoms in gentle gratitude. Do not desecrate Her by

vile thoughts, sounds or emotions, or by physical acts that despoil Her virgin beauty. Honor the Earth, "the Mother" that is hosting your evolutionary pathway.

7. Do not form nor offer opinions unless invited to do so, and then, only after prayer and silent invocation for guidance. Speak when God chooses to say something through you. At other times it is best to speak little, or to remain peacefully silent.

8. Let your heart sing a song of gratitude and joy unto God. Be grateful always for all that you have received and that you have in the now moment. Tap in to the River of Life, River of Love and Abundance that lies within the Sacred Heart.

9. In speech and action be gentle, but with the dignity that always accompanies the Presence of the living God that lives within the temple of your being. Constantly place all the faculties of your being and all the inner unfoldment of your nature at the feet of the God-power, endeavoring to manifest the perfection of compassion when meeting those in distress.

10. Let your word be spoken in gentleness, humility, and loving service. Do not allow the impression of humility to be mistaken for lethargy, for the servant of the Lord, like the sun in the heavens, is eternally vigilant and constantly outpouring the gifts of Love to those who open their hearts to receive them.

Meditation

Journey to the Crystal-Rose Flame Temple of Love

Adama with Paul the Venetian

This is one of the etheric temples of the Love Ray, guarded and maintained by the Love Flame of the archangels of the Third Ray, Chamuel and Charity. It is situated over St. Louis, Missouri, on the south side of North America. An arc of divine love forms a bridge between this retreat and that of the Elohim of the Third Ray, Heros and Amora, in the etheric realm near Lake Winnipeg in Canada.

The emanation of the Love Ray from this specific temple is a flow of creativity. The Flame of Love from this retreat promotes the generosity of the heart, givingness, forgiveness and mercy. The enormous energy of Love simply flushes out all else and assists the people who visit this temple to retain more of the qualities of Love for themselves and for the world. The altar and flame of the retreat are dedicated to the flow of life from the heart of the Creator to the heart of Christ and then to the heart of man.

Now, my beloveds, come with me, accompanied by the energy of the Holy Spirit through the love of the Master Paul the Venetian, to that specific Temple of Love. Close your eyes and take a few deep breaths. Set your intention to come with us in the etheric vehicle we now present to you. You come in your light body vehicle. You may or may not have a conscious remembrance of this, but the benefits are the same. Use the gift of your imagination to create a vivid impression of what we are presenting you with, and the journey will remain imprinted in your soul and cellular memory. When needed, you will be able to access, not

The Third Ray

necessarily the recollection of all the details, but certainly the energies that you will receive through this experience.

Also know that the more you take these types of journeys, the more you assist the thinning of your own veil of illusion that blocks your memories and your perceptions of the higher vibrations. Ask your Higher Self to facilitate this journey for you and with you, and open your heart to make this happen on the inner planes at the highest level possible.

We are now traveling through space from your home in Mount Shasta to the magnificent Crystal-Rose Flame Temple of Love. Feel the fragrance of the crystal-rose petals of love flowing all around you, even before you arrive. You are so very blessed, for a small group to have the privilege of being accompanied personally by the planetary representative of the Holy Spirit Himself, is indeed, a rare occurrence. Let me share with all of you now here present in this room that it is your love and your staunch devotion for your pathway which allows Him to grant you this grace.

Breathe in, my beloveds. Relax into the experience fully. Deepen your breath to allow you to bring back the greatest soul imprint you can create. This will assist you to enhance your pathway in a more harmonious and direct way. *(Short pause)*

We have now arrived in front of that large translucent crystal-rose, multi-layered dome. It is nothing like you have ever seen in your outer world. There are no words in the vocabulary of your language to describe the structure, so beautiful and elegant, fashioned by the creativity of the archangelic love of Chamuel and Charity.

Beam Rays of pure Love energy emanate from the central point of the dome to radiate the Love of the Creator hundreds of miles into the atmosphere in all directions. A most wondrous scene to behold, dear ones!

Allow yourself to walk on the velvety crystal-rose carpet that extends beneath your feet to the doorway of the temple. Because we are in the company of the Maha Chohan Himself, you will not be required to show your passport of entry to be admitted here. Because archangelic frequencies are so high and rarified, no souls are permitted to come here unless they are able to maintain fourth dimensional frequencies of love and harmony at all times, and are accompanied by one of the Masters of Wisdom.

As you get close to the entranceway, several angels of the Love Ray, about 12 feet tall, bow to the great Light of the Maha Chohan. They also bow to my Light and to your own Light, bidding you entrance.

Each of you is escorted by one of the temple guardians. This temple is three times larger than the Vatican of the Catholic Church in Rome and contains many sections of various dimensional energies for the numerous activities of the temple.

You are taken to an area which will be comfortable for your own level of heart evolution. You are now crossing a long corridor filled with thousands of love-flame angels of all sizes. These angelic beings vary from the smallest cherubim to the largest seraphim. Actually, all twelve choirs of the angelic kingdom from all dimensions are represented here.

As you walk the corridor, a large number of fountains and cascades of pure Love energy spring forth from various places. The energies that emanate from these fountains and cascades sing songs of Love and Gratitude perpetually to the heart of the Creator, to the Divine Mother and to all kingdoms evolving

The Third Ray

on the planet, in all dimensions. This also includes surface humanity. If you allow it, these melodies of Love can melt much of the dross accumulated in the heart over a long time. Listen and let your hearts merge with the energies of the love songs coming out of the Waters of the Eternal Rivers of Love.

Pure white doves of Love, much larger than the ones you know on the surface, send you their healing radiance. Take your time to look, feel and observe the wonders of God's Love waiting to be bestowed upon those who love Life and obey the Eternal Laws of Love. No one is rushing you. Remember, you are here in a zone of timelessness. Also listen to the love songs of the many varieties of Third Ray flowers, plants and fruit gracing this temple pathway. Allow yourself to receive healing from the sweetness of the fragrance and melodies. The doves also want to connect with your heart to offer comfort on your journey back to the "Sun of your Presence." Walking this corridor which portrays the energies of magical pure Love is part of your experience here. If you have any questions, each of you have your own angelic guide waiting to answer. *(Pause)*

See now an entrance on the right. Your guides are bidding you to follow them into the Hall of the Eternal Flame of Cosmic Love. This is another unfed Flame that is perpetually burning to glorify the Creator, the Father of All. By cosmic law, all planets receiving the love and energies of the Creator must return to Him a portion each day, produced by the fire of those hearts who inhabit these planets. On this planet, since surface humanity has neglected to do this for eons of time while journeying in war and separation, we in Telos, and many beings from the Inner Earth and other subterranean cities have done this on your behalf. We are going to continue doing this until the day that all of you attain enough spiritual maturity to return that level of grace and gratitude to the Creator yourself.

Those serving in the Crystal-Rose Temple as their service rendered to Life, also feed the Eternal Flame of Love through the love fires of their hearts. When we say unfed Flame, we mean the element that nourishes and keeps the Flame burning perpetually from the fire of Love of those who serve in that temple. In fact, all actions combined with the other Temples of Love holding the same energy create a web of Light that nourishes all civilizations and the various kingdoms living on Earth.

This Flame, ever so gentle and powerful, stands a hundred feet and more in height and about 9 feet in diameter. The source of its strength is the power of gentleness. It is blissful, joyous and playful, containing all the many blessings the Creator wishes to bestow on His Creation and to the many children of His heart. Its bounty is limitless.

Take time now to breathe it in even more deeply. Connect deeply with the Flame, allowing it to fill your heart to the brim; and relax in the arms of Love. How wondrous! *(Pause)*

When you feel that your heart has been filled to full capacity, you can quietly return to the crystal merkaba waiting outside to bring you back to your physical body. In deep gratitude, thank Paul the Venetian for the Grace he has accorded you today, and in the future for those who will be working with the written material. When you are ready, open your eyes and come back to your body.

With these words, we now conclude our meditation. I urge you to return there in consciousness whenever you feel that you need to boost the fires of your heart to a greater degree. I bring you much love from Telos; our love for you is pure and unconditional, ready to accompany your step into the end of your journey.

The Third Ray

Aurelia - *On behalf of the group here, I thank you Adama very profoundly for all that you do for us, and I also thank Paul the Venetian for the Love, the Grace and the Blessings He has bestowed upon us today. We feel so privileged daily to receive this information first hand. I am very grateful!*

Adama - You are welcome, my beloveds!

The Seven Sacred Flames

Lord Serapis Bey

Chapter Four

The Fourth Ray:

The Ascension Flame of Purification

Main God qualities and actions of the Fourth Ray:
Purity, wholeness, Christ consciousness and becoming God through the consciousness of the Divine Mother.

Corresponding Chakra: Base of the Spine
Color: White
Corresponding Stones: Azurite, Snow quartz

Chohan of the Fourth Ray:
Lord Serapis Bey
His Retreat: The Great Hall of Ascension
Temple at Luxor, Egypt

Archangels of the Fourth Ray with Divine Complement:
Gabriel and Hope
Their Retreat: Between Sacramento and Mount Shasta, CA, USA

Elohim of the Fourth Ray with Divine Complement:
Purity and Astrea
Their Retreat: Near Gulf of Archangels, Russia

About Lord Serapis Bey

Lord Serapis Bey is Chohan of the Fourth Ray, guardian of the Ascension Flame. He is the disciplinarian, known through the centuries for his strict discipline. Real discipline is not control over another to thwart innate progress, but instead holds in check the human qualities to allow the Real Self to have expression. This is essential for the attainment of Ascension which is the culmination of all embodiments. He is devoted to the perfection of the soul through compassion, patience, understanding and self-discipline. He assists all who call upon him in the development of the intuitive and creative faculties of the heart. Lord Serapis Bey can be called upon to open your eyes to the beauty of God's creations. He assists all who call upon him in expressing their most heart-felt creative aspects.

Embodiments of Lord Serapis Bey

- Serapis Bey was embodied as a high priest in the Ascension Temple on Atlantis more than 11,500 years ago. He is the one who brought the Ascension Flame from Atlantis to Egypt just prior to the destruction of that continent.

- Serapis Bey spent many lifetimes along the Nile, and as the Egyptian pharaoh Amenhotep III, (1417-1379 BC), he was called "the Magnificent."He brought Egypt to the height of diplomatic prestige, prosperity and peace. His extensive building of monuments, palaces and temples included construction of the Temple of Luxor.

- His most familiar incarnation was Leonidas, King of Sparta, the great warrior who led the Spartans in the famous battle at Thermopylae, Greece.

- Serapis Bey ascended around 400 B.C.

The Fourth Ray

The Temple of Luxor

In the land of Egypt, along the banks of the Nile River, there exists the focus of the Great White Brotherhood dedicated to preserving the Cosmic Flame of Ascension. The Ascension Temple at Luxor sustains the pulsation of the Ascension Flame in the atmosphere of Earth. Those of the human race who awaken in each century with the desire to complete the cycles of incarnation become the responsibility of the Ascension Brotherhood. Their service to Life is to create the opportunity of necessary initiations for the neophytes who come to Luxor to qualify for Ascension. Serapis Bey, Lord of Love, explains that Luxor provides the opportunity for spiritual development.

The Ascension Flame at Luxor and the one generated in Telos, both hold the same frequencies and are available for the people of Earth. This flame is utilizerd freely by the nature kingdom in its resurrection each successive season of spring.

From Lord Serapis Bey: *The candidate for Ascension must meet "seven major initiations." The candidate must successfully pass through the disciplines of the Seven Great Temples.*

"I am embodied discipline," says Serapis Bey. For centuries most people have feared that discipline. I am dedicated to seeing that you pass through the fires of purification, and that you, who desire the opportunity of gaining your ascension, might persevere until the day of that victory. Angels of the Ascension Temple gather all the praise, adoration, songs, devotion and blessings sent upward by individuals in congregational or individual worship. These energies created by devotional practices are carefully woven into the ever-widening spiritual stream of energy. Each new soul who attains Ascension status makes it easier for the next lifestream to avail itself of the fully-gathered cosmic momentum of those who have gone before.

First: The candidate must learn to control and transform all thoughts and feelings that are not aligned with their Divine Self. This is the initiation of mastery of the first temple, the Temple of God's Will that the hopeful and the brave must pass. The candidate must learn to commune with his own God Presence and to develop within himself true humility before it. Within this first temple, under the direction of Master El Morya and his assistants, the aspirant is assisted in the dissolving of rebellion. Rebellion took Lucifer from the heart of heaven; the rebellion against discipline and self-correction is a barrier to real spiritual progress. Within the discipline of a good night's sleep, abstinence from tobacco, alcohol and recreational drugs, you ease your pathway to your glorious freedom. Those who do not wish to accept those disciplines have not yet the stimulus to become the best, to be the highest and the greatest expression of a God incarnate.

Second: Those who have successfully passed the initiations of the first temple are taken to the second temple, known as the Temple of Learning. Under the guidance of Lord Lanto, the Master Kuthumi and the Brotherhood of the Golden Robe, they are given instructions in the Law. Here they develop understanding of the Law of cause and effect and all other Universal Laws. It is a pleasant and happy time of sowing the seeds, of breathing life upon those seeds and bringing in a harvest of work. It is the time when the artist develops his skills, the musician develops dexterity in his musical accomplishments and the teacher becomes eloquent in conveying knowledge to his students.

Third: Those who have successfully passed the initiations of the second temple are taken to the third temple, the Temple of Love, under the great protection and guidance of the Beloved Paul the Venetian. Here the neophyte must learn the discipline of unconditional love and harmony for their own lifestream and for all other forms of Life. They are placed in living quarters with those who have within themselves tendencies which are particularly aggravating to others. This is where the numbers of neophytes dwindle, and with great feeling of relief, many candidates rush to the door and leave us. To live peacefully with one's fellowmen is one of the greatest tests of the unascended state. Although the graciousness, the beauty, the kindliness of this great Master are so astonishing as to melt a heart of stone, the discipline he requires in learning tolerance, compassion and understanding is such that few survive.

Fourth: From the third temple, the initiate moves into the fourth temple, the Temple of Ascension. This is the first personal contact that Serapis Bey has with the neophyte. For the first time, the candidate must draw forth enough purity to see his I AM Presence and his Holy Christ Self face-to-face. In the initiation, the Master himself will stand within the aura of the initiate presenting many negative imbalances which still exist within the inner bodies. This is when the candidate will hear many voices and only true discrimination, prayer, selflessness and humility can discern the "Voice of the Silence." It is the time when the "Self" is shown the tricks of the ego and subtle appearances. The aspirant must apply himself to purify all past negative human creations and transform them into pure-white Light Radiance.

Fifth: After passing the initiation of the fourth temple, the disciple is ready for the discipline of the fifth temple, the Temple of Consecration. It is then that the garment of consecration is placed upon them, golden sandals on their feet and a silken robe on their body. Master Hilarion or Beloved Raphael performs the service of consecration where all body systems are consecrated to purity and ascension. Then consecrations are given, of the hands into which the Flame of Healing is infused, and of the feet which become the anchors of the Sacred Fire wherever the body moves. Consecration of the lips takes place to speak the Sacred Words which invoke and command the manifestation of precipitation and healing powers. Consecration of the energies of the eyes enables the disciple to see perfection and to call it forth. This completes the ceremonies.

Sixth: The aspirant is then taken to the sixth temple, the Temple of Service where he is expected to temporarily put aside his worldly pursuits to be in service to others and to become his brother's keeper. He is also expected to volunteer some of his time to planetary service for the benefit of mankind, not just himself and his family. He must learn to include the rest of humanity in his heart, becoming fully aware that the needs of others also affect the needs of many. In the sixth temple, under the sponsorship of Lord Sananda with his beloved twin flame, Nada *(also known as Jesus and Mary Magdalene),* the aspirant is trained to nurture and serve all aspects of Life and become a ministering servant.

Before a candidate for ascension can become a master, he must also learn the disciplines of the humble servant, selfless service, true brotherhood and obedience to Hierarchy. Those spending almost their entire lives in the service of some activity or organization to assist and enhance the consciousness of the collective are usually sixth level initiates. In the past, too often, Serapis Bey saw many of you leave Luxor, ready to set the world on fire, only to recede back as you went down the steps of the great temple. This is where a great number of you lost your opportunity for Ascension in many incarnations.

Seventh: After the aspirant passes the initiations of the first six temples, he is ready to enter the seventh temple, the Temple of the Violet Fire where every atom, cell and electron of his being becomes completely purified by the action of the Violet Flame under the sponsorship of Master Saint Germain. The candidate becomes like a window through which the God-life flows with absolute purity. The physical body will give you the greatest possible ease and grace within the Laws of harmony, if you refrain from taking into the physical body those substances which change its natural vibratory action, disconnecting it from the harmony of the spheres of Divine Love. When the candidate is ready to fully externalize the Will of God, and preparations begin to initiate the final phase of the graduation ceremony of Ascension, then all is in place for the candidate to become an "ascended master." Do you see? Blessings from the heart of Luxor!

Transmission from the Heart of Lord Serapis Bey, the Lord of Love

Beloved Brothers and Sisters of Earth, with the great Love of my Heart, I send to each one who reads this material the blessings of Luxor and of Telos. Realize, beloved ones, that never in the history of the Earth, has the opportunity for humanity to attain the freedom of their glorious Ascension been offered with so much ease and grace in this wondrous time of preparation for your planet's Ascension. An exceptional window of opportunity is presented to those of humanity who wish to gain their spiritual freedom and who are willing to do whatever it takes to make it happen.

I am not proclaiming that it will be entirely easy for everyone. My promise to you is that I and the large teams of the Ascension Brotherhood of Luxor and of Telos stand ready to support and coach with much love and compassion those who will seriously commit to their evolution. Yes, many of you will face temporary challenges from time to time, but if you face them with surrender, devotion, joy, enthusiasm, and the attitude of gratitude for the exceptional opportunity offered to you at this time, be assured that the rest of your path does not have to be difficult.

It all has to do with the perceptions and reactions you feel regarding what presents itself in your life as an opportunity to align past karma and integrate the lessons you need to learn in order to become an Ascended Master. Though the initiations are basically the same for everyone, they manifest in a different way for each lifestream according to the unique pathway and one's own level of initiation and evolution.

Know, beloved ones, that once you have made a serious commitment to your Ascension, all heaven is at your beck and call to assist you in a most wondrous way. In former times, the Ascension was extremely difficult to attain. With the new dispensation now given to humanity by your Creator, the pathway basically remains the same, but you now have so much more assistance available to you and so much more information that those in the past did not have access to.

Luxor and Telos are waiting for your return. Most of you have come to both places many times, but many of you left, fearing that it would be too difficult. And you are still here on the surface of Earth, often in pain and despair. Realize that the temporary difficulties on the path are so much easier to bear than the lifetimes of pain and struggle you experienced once you embraced the illusion that you could not do it.

In fact, I say to all of you that if you are really serious about ascending in this life and if you apply all the Laws of Love with absolute constancy and perseverance, "you can do it." With our help and with the help of your "I AM Presence" and your "Higher Mental Body," nothing is impossible. In fact, it is not only possible but most desirable for your evolution that you do not stay behind in the third dimension very long after the Earth's Ascension around 2012. This is my promise to you that we will match your efforts in assisting each one of you. We love you all very dearly and our dedication to assist you is so absolute! Once you discover the real truth about Ascension, you will no longer hesitate to let go of the outmoded lifestyles you have accepted as "normal," and prepare yourself to live as a true Child of God.

On behalf of those of the Ascension Brotherhood of Luxor who serve with me in that Holy Purpose of holding the Sacred Energies of the Ascension Flame, we send to all of you who read our words of Wisdom, our deepest Love and Mantle of Peace. I AM Serapis Bey from the Ascension Temple of Luxor!

The Seven Sacred Flames

Base (Root) Chakra

The Fourth Ray

Prayer for Fourth Ray Healing

Prayer for Personal Ascension

In the name of my beloved God-Presence "I AM." I ask to receive the initiations needed to qualify for Ascension. I call for a great cosmic shaft of Cosmic Purity Flame to remove from my mind, my thoughts, my feelings and my body, and all subtle bodies every vibration of human creation that is impure in substance and less than my Divine Perfection in God.

May the Flame of Purity transmute from my world
all remaining negative energies!
May the Love of Christ expand in me
through the power of the Ascension Flame!
May the Resurrection Flame awaken the memories
of my divine blueprint.
So that I can be free forever from all discord
that I have ever created!

I affirm that I AM Purity in action.
I AM God's Purity established within mind, body and soul.
Let me also invoke Purity for every part of Life on Earth.
Let me invoke Purity for my family,
my friends and for the whole family of God,
all Kingdoms and the Earth.
And so it is, beloved I AM!

Discourse from Adama with Serapis Bey

Peace and love from the Heart of Lemuria, this is Adama with the Chohan of the Fourth Ray, our beloved Serapis Bey. I bring you the blessings of my Light and the victory that lies within it. We are bidding you our most heartfelt welcome.

Today, we wish to talk about the Ascension Flame, a most wondrous action of the sacred fire that can facilitate your pathway to your goal of ascension. When you possess a more specific understanding of how to consciously use this glorious Flame of purification, you can accelerate the cleansing process of all your chakras, the activation of your DNA and prepare the cells of your various bodies for a physical ascension. This is magnificent, my friends, to say the least.

Lord Serapis Bey came today with his team of masters who have specialized in that service. They are known as "The Ascension Brotherhood of Luxor." These masters extend to you now the elixir of their heart's love through the purifying fires of the Ascension Flame. Breathe this in, my beloveds; this is a gift to you. These dedicated beings have worked closely with our brother Serapis for several centuries, planning the evolution of the human race for the time that has finally come. Their service to Life consists of the engagement of their energies in preparing for the lifting of our planet and the consciousness of humanity for planetary ascension in the years to come.

The Ascension Temple at Luxor sustains the pulsation of the Ascension Flame in the atmosphere of Earth, as does our Ascension Temple in Telos. Visualize two temples, united in consciousness and in energy, blessing and loving daily and hourly everything on Earth for the benefit of ascending humanity. With each successive spring season, this Sacred Flame is

The Fourth Ray

freely and widely utilized by the beings of the nature kingdom to assist the renewal and resurrection of the beauty of Nature. Each soul on Earth desiring to complete their cycle of incarnations by the process of Ascension is placed under the tutelage of the Ascension Brotherhood and of the Office of the Christ.

A couple of hundred years ago, a great portion of the activities and records that this great pyramid held for so long in Luxor was either transferred or duplicated in Telos. The relocation of records was implemented then, because the spiritual hierarchy of the planet could foresee future potential problems in that area of the globe. The records and energies of that sacred focus could not be compromised in the event of regional or global cataclysms that were on the horizon then. So now, Telos has become the main focus of Ascension for this planet in total union and cooperation with the great masters of Luxor. We all work together in perfect harmony for the benefit of the collective. This is one of the fifth dimensional protocols.

The decision was made that the records of this important planetary focus would be safer underground, and best guarded in its original purity and sacredness, nurtured and honored by a large number of ascended beings such as those of us in Telos.

Although it may seem that there are now two main Ascension focuses on the planet, I say that for us, it is only one. In the dimension where we function, time and space, as most of you understand it, do not exist, and all is one.

After the sinking of Atlantis and Lemuria, the surface populations have continued to war against each other until this day. Keep the hope and your courage, my beloveds. Know that it will not be tolerated much longer, and this consciousness will soon come to an end and be healed.

In Telos, soon after the destruction of both continents, we volunteered for the task of keeping the Flame of Ascension on behalf of mankind as our service to this planet, in order to insure its continuity. From the Love of our Hearts, we extend to you this day your opportunity to embrace and expand this wondrous Flame within your hearts for your own Ascension. We say that the heart ascends first, and then the rest follows.

Aurelia - *Will a large percentage of humanity ascend by 2012?*

Adama - It is not yet known how many people will ascend with the planet by the year 2012. We perceive a potential of a few million out of 7 billion people on the planet, but this number is subject to change any time according to individual and collective choices. We often hear those calling themselves "lightworkers" say that, by the year 2012, all humanity will ascend to the fifth dimension unconditionally, and that no one will be left behind. And we say back to you, "Not so." No one will be left behind ultimately, but everyone must do their own inner work first and evolve their consciousness before being invited to the great "Hall of Ascension."

Although there is greater assistance offered to humanity than ever before in Earth's history, and the Ascension process is made easier than ever before, none of you will be lifted into the Ascension process until you have met all the requirements and reached this frequency in your consciousness, no matter how long it takes in the cycles of time.

It will be required of those aspiring for Ascension that you heal and transform all your erroneous belief systems and embrace love, harmlessness and the truth of your divinity. Realize that the year 2012 is not the end of the ascension cycle on this planet, but simply a wondrous beginning. The full planetary process for the Earth, in the completion of Her full glory and destiny is a 2,000-year plan. In 2012, it is the Earth, Herself, making her Ascension in the Light, along with those who have met all the necessary requirements.

In the years following 2012, all souls incarnated on Earth will continue their evolution and ascend only when they are ready at the soul level. For some it may take six months, others five to eight years and for many, it will be longer. You will also need to engage yourself seriously in the initiation process leading to ascension. Each one's journey is unique, and though the initiatic process is similar for everyone, it unfolds differently for each soul, according to their own distinctive pathway.

It is true that everyone, without exception, is offered the opportunity for Ascension at this time, but not everyone is choosing it. Those beloved souls who choose to continue to experience separation or are not yet ready for this evolutionary step will be given the opportunity to continue their evolution at their own pace somewhere else. The grace of Ascension will be offered to them again at some later time when they request it. In time, everyone will return to the frequency of the Love of the Heart of the Creator. In this way, no one will be left behind.

Aurelia - *Adama, would you give us a description of this Flame?*

Adama - This Flame contains the frequency and color of all the other Flames. You see or experience it as a brilliant, luminous, white dazzling light that consumes on contact all that is less than the perfection of Love. Its power and brilliance are limitless, sustaining worlds in perfect harmony and beauty.

Those invoking and working with it must prepare for change. Once touched by that Flame, you are never the same again. Everyone can work with it, of course, but in its full intensity, it holds the capacity to completely transform the initiate who has reached the doorway of Ascension. When you are finally ready to take this leap in your evolution, you will be immersed in the frequency of that magnificent energy. It will propel you into the final step, when the fires of that Love will consume all human limitations, your full consciousness will be restored and all your bodies will align and unite. You will then be invited to join the "immortals," as an ascended master. You will step into that glorious spiritual freedom and consciously reconnect with your Creator and with all that exists within His heart. This is, my friends, how powerful the Ascension Flame is.

Aurelia - *How can we consciously reach and maintain this level of frequency?*

Adama - This information has been given to people of Earth again and again, but it has been ignored; in this age, it is given again through a wide variety of writings and channelings. It has been presented to you simply in so many packages and colors that you fail to recognize it.

Unless a teaching and key of wisdom is learned thoroughly and integrated through the heart, it remains "just information" and clutter in your mind soon forgotten. Ultimately, it does not advance the evolution of your consciousness. We know people who have read hundreds of spiritual books; they have acquired mental knowledge, but when this knowledge is not integrated to embody their divinity, spiritual progress remains marginal.

Allow me to mention to you briefly again, repeating what has been said before, in the hope that if repeated often enough, it will eventually sink in. "Ascension" does not require the doing of so many things, but is all about becoming, embracing and remembering to live your lives as the God/Goddess that you are. It means fully embracing the divinity that already exists within you through the expansion of your consciousness as

Beings of Love, and living from the wisdom of the heart. It is that simple, my beloveds. If you become this, you do not need anything else. All this already exists and lives within you. I remind you that there is nothing outside the Self.

Here are some of the main points or guidelines to be understood and considered about the initiatic path leading to your graduation from Earth's curriculum through the Ascension protocols.

- This process is one of complete purification and healing of all that is hindering your transfiguration, resurrection and ascension into the arms of God/Love; the restoration of your dignity and memories, so that you live, once again, as divine children of your heavenly Father/Creator, entering the world of "Oneness."

- Understand that each dimension represents a certain frequency. The fifth dimension becomes accessible to you when, and only when, you have attained that frequency in your consciousness and have the ability to maintain it at all times.

- Live from the heart, talking and acting like a master would, as a way of "being." Always ask yourself the questions, "What would a master do or say in this and that situation?" Then go within and find the answer. If it is not clear, take a piece of paper and pen, light a candle if you wish, and set your intention to find the answer inside of you. The master within is awake and alert at all times, forever waiting for your recognition.

- Let go of the third dimensional consciousness of separation, duality, polarity and drama in all its myriad forms. Stop believing in two powers, and giving your power and precious energy to the illusion of this 3D density. Allow yourself to set aside all that you learned so far that has not given you the results you are yearning for. Be ready and willing to learn anew and have the courage to step into the unknown reality of Love and Magic. Recognize that Love is the only true power there is, and start living your life in that vibrational frequency from the inside out.

- Let go of all judgment and expectations about yourself and others, and how life should be unfolding for you. Allow yourself to perceive and embrace all the wonders and majesty of "YOU" in the splendor of your divinity, and accept the great adventure of letting it unfold and transform in front of your eyes, in deep joy and gratitude.

- Embrace the banner of humility and the sweet surrender to one's holy vows. If you don't know what they are, they are written within your very cells and DNA, as well as in many chambers of your Sacred Heart. Be willing to take the time to go within and investigate.

- Establish a conscious union with your I AM Presence and the fulfillment of your divine plan. The ascension is the unification, the merging into divine union with your magnificent I AM Presence. In order to embody this glorious aspect of yourself, it is an obvious requirement that you make yourself very familiar and intimate with that aspect of Self you want to merge with. How can you expect to ascend and unify with an aspect of Self that you have not spent the time to know and understand?

When we ask people through channeling sessions what the ascension means to them, we are amazed at the answers we receive, such as changing dimension, being able to manifest everything, not having to be limited by money anymore, being able to teleport, and so on. Although these become the gifts and results of ascension, they are not its primary purpose. YOU, your level of understanding your divinity and becoming it brings it forth.

- Embrace the consciousness of harmlessness by honoring the sanctity of all life sharing this planet with you, and also the divine right of every person to live here as well.

- Release old programming running your life and all negative emotions stored in your conscious, unconscious and subconscious memories, including the balancing of all debts incurred towards life. You have already received many teachings on these topics.

- When individuals believe their debt to be light and they enter into the spirit of releasing it steadily into the sacred fire, they create a great release of joy that flows through their being. The feeling of joy within your consciousness has a tendency to create malleability in the coil of energy that keeps the records of the debts, relaxing tensions within the energetic coils, and freeing the individual to move on more quickly through all initiations with greater ease and grace.

- The attitudes that most assist anyone to move through the balancing of their shadow creation are twofold. First, adopt, as a way of life, each moment of the day, "as an act of love," for yourself, for your fellowmen, for the planet, for other kingdoms sharing the planet with you and in gratitude for creation itself. And secondly, practicing the attitude of gratitude will assist you immensely.

- Nurture and expand a genuine desire for your ascension and immortality, embracing the willingness to walk the path unto the end! Unless you entertain a genuine desire for ascension and immortality, unless you are willing to shed the old ways of living in the third dimension that has kept you and humanity in pain, and walk the path shown to you by the Masters of Wisdom who have tread the way before you, you cannot become a true candidate for Ascension on the inner planes.

In seeking Ascension, the power of Love must become the fervent heat which will cause the elements of mortal creation to melt, and which will propel the candidate for Ascension into the great cosmic pool of immortal Love and Light.

Message from Serapis Bey

For those calling themselves seekers of truth who yearn for contacts with the Hierarchy of Light and the Great White Brotherhood, it is required that you come directly under the guidance and the tutelage of the great master teachers. The path of mastery, achievement, freedom, victory and ascension can only be gained through the initiatic process. For all great masters who have ever ascended from this planet, or elsewhere, the Flame of Ascension has always remained a most important key which unlocks the door of immortality for every soul.

I have guarded, guided and stood within the Ascension Flame for a very long time, in order that there might be a way and means by which humanity, when through with their folly of the senses, could return to their Divine tate. Since the "fall of man," if there had not been a guarding Brotherhood of the Ascension Flame, there would be no way back home for humanity. Have you ever pondered within the deepest recesses of your being what it would be like if there were no way back home?

To this end, many of us have remained prisoners of Love upon this temporary dark Star. The Lemurian Brotherhood of Light of Telos joined us in our vigil of Ascension for the planet. Together, we kept the Flame of Love and Light on behalf of mankind for thousands of years, until such a day when you have acquired enough spiritual maturity to partake in this planetary responsibility.

I am dedicated to see that you pass through the fires of purification and that you, who have applied for the opportunity of attaining the ascended status, will remain firm and vigilant in your commitment until that glorious victory becomes your reality. We are heart-friends of many ages.

Quote from Lord Jesus/Sananda

"Knowing the supreme glory of that hour, I can but urge each dear child of God to prepare for that glorious moment! When the hour comes and the summons from the Father of Light reaches your heart, you will also know the full and true purpose for human incarnations. It is to prepare your consciousness to become a Sun of Light within yourself, free of the wheel of birth and death, and a master of energy and vibration."

Those interested in visiting the Ascension Temples at Luxor and Telos are requested to bring back in their consciousness that rising, buoyant, joyous energy which is the activity of Ascension. This Flame will enter into the elemental substance of the inner bodies, as well as the physical form, and act as the "leaven in the loaf," when earnestly invoked. As the pure white Flame passes through the substance of the aspirant's bodies—physical, mental, emotional and etheric—it quickens the vibratory action of the atom, each electron moving more rapidly around its own central pole. This causes the throwing off of the impure, discordant substances around the electron, and quickens the rhythm of all the vehicles.

To ascend to the state of self-mastery, God wisdom, peace, harmony, perfect health, limitlessness, and ever-present supply, the candidate for the great gift of Ascension must learn to rely totally upon the Presence of God within the heart. The disciplines of the Ascension Brotherhood are designed to turn the consciousness from the outer world "inward," until, from within the heart center, the seat of your divinity, there is drawn forth and at will anything and everything which is required to manifest the fullness of your Divine Essence in physical manifestation. All must be purified and transformed through the ascending fires of that royal, dazzling, purifying Flame!

Meditation

Journey to the Ascension Temple in Telos

With Adama and Lord Serapis Bey

Along with our honorable guests here this evening, twelve members of the Ascension Brotherhood of Luxor, we now invite you to come with us on a journey to the Ascension Temple of Telos. If you desire this initiation, like a master, set your intention in your heart with your Higher Self and guides to come along with us for this experience.

A dazzling white light merkaba from the fifth dimension is now approaching to take, in their etheric bodies, those who choose to come. With intention, step into that vehicle of light and take your seat. We ask you to start preparing yourself by centering within, and allowing yourself to feel and to perceive the buoyant and joyous energies of this Flame already enfolding you. We ask that through this journey, you breathe as deeply

The Fourth Ray

as you can, in order to return as much of the energies of this Flame to your outer awareness. This experience is another opportunity to ignite for yourself the next level of the purification process for every cell, atom and electron of your physical and all subtle bodies.

Youp! Since we are not very far away, we are already there. Open yourself to this experience as consciously as you can, and enjoy! This temple is built as a huge, very tall scintillating white light pyramid with four sides. If you have been to the one in Egypt, you will notice that it is not exactly the same, but similar in many ways. Of course, the fifth dimensional aspects of those two ascension pyramids are so much more glorious, elegant and magnificent in nature than the outer one visible to your eyes in Egypt. The one in Telos does not have a third dimensional counterpart as at Luxor, and its power and beauty are stunning.

Step off the merkaba and follow us to the "Hall of Ascension," where each one of you will be introduced to the Ascension Brotherhood guide who will escort you during your experience here. Feel the air, the energies, the power and the brilliance of this holy place. We also encourage you to pay attention to your guide and ask any question you want clarity on. This is your experience, beloveds, and you create it in any way you wish. Our role is simply to accompany you with our love and wisdom.

At times, you are almost blinded by such brilliance, and this is good. You are now walking through a corridor of exquisite beauty, leading to the atomic accelerator chamber. Continue to fill your lungs and consciousness with this beauty and joy. As you walk along, there are many beings who serve in this temple or are visiting here, who notice you and greet you with their smiles and gestures of friendship. All of them, in their own way, welcome you and send you their blessings. The halls of this temple are usually open only for those whose candidature for ascension has been accepted.

The guardians of the atomic accelerator chamber bid you welcome and you are now entering this great hall with your guide. What you see is a very large room that contains several hundred small dazzling white crystalline pyramids circling the main focus of that Flame in the center of the room. You are almost overtaken by the wonder and magnificence of the immortal unfed Flame of Ascension burning bright in front of you, almost 200 feet tall and 100 feet in diameter at the base.

Its power almost overwhelms you and you know that once you have had a deep experience of this Flame you will never quite be the same again, unless you consciously choose to return to your former level of resonance. In spite of its great rushing power, it does not emit any noise, except the melodious sounds of music that is created by this energy field. Also notice the sweet fragrance that facilitates the raising of your frequency emanating from the energies of the Ascension Flame.

With your guide, you now walk around the base of the Flame to fill yourself with all the spiritual gifts that you can receive here today. Your guide, who has already chosen one of the smaller pyramids for you, invites you to step in for your next experience. Each one of these small pyramids of light contains an atomic activator, on which you sit comfortably, that will assist in raising your vibration to a level that is comfortable for you. These accelerators have been designed in such a way that they could raise you to the Ascension frequency and immortality, but this is not the goal of this experience. You are truly here to experience "a little push" to your next level that is different for each one. The level of acceleration each one receives is calibrated to their level of initiation and readiness on their pathway.

The Fourth Ray

As much as some of you would love to experience the full Ascension at this time, you will not disappear. We guarantee you that you will return to your physical bodies in good shape and charged with a new and purer vibration in your auric field. It will be up to you, from now on, to use this experience to the best of your ability as another step forward, or forget quickly what you have gained and maintain the status quo. We are only your facilitators.

What is an atomic accelerator? For those of you not yet familiar with this concept that Master Saint Germain has spoken about in his channelings of the last century, let us describe it briefly. He is one of the designers of this technology. The atomic accelerator does exactly what its name says. It is a crystalline seat or chair designed with a technology that creates the frequency of the Ascension Flame for those sitting on it. Like many of your instruments, it possesses a dial of control, and as you meditate on this Flame and pour the love of your heart into it, you are infused by your guide with this frequency at the exact level that best serves you in the now moment. Your guides already know the frequency that is best for you, and they are well trained in applying it.

This type of technology is not available yet in your dimension. It has the ability to transform into perfection every element that vibrates at a frequency less than the purest Love essence of the Creator. One can really and symbolically say that it has the ability to transform base metals into the purest gold. In other words, when the time comes for you to make your Ascension, it will transform your mortal body with all its imperfections and limitations into your immortal deathless solar body of light, with the majesty and splendor that come with it.

As you continue to sit on the seat assigned to you, keep breathing while communing with your Divine Essence and with your

Creator. Set your goals of Ascension for this life and open your heart to your God. *(Pause for integration)*

When you feel complete, look into the eyes of your guide and receive the love that he imparts to you through the eyes of his soul and express your gratitude. When you feel ready, stand up and direct your consciousness to exit, with your guide, the chamber you are in, and retrace your steps back to the merkaba that brought you here. We are now taking you back to Aurelia's home with your auric fields and hearts filled with a new love and a new light vibration. It is up to you to maintain, nurture and expand it.

Now come back to full consciousness in your body and offer your gratitude to God for the opportunity and gift you have just received, and be blissfully joyous. We love you most profoundly, and this love accompanies you each day of your life.

The Atomic Accelerator/Ascension Chair
A Tool for Creating a Chalice of Light

Greetings, beloveds, this is Adama with Master Saint Germain. I would like to talk to you about the atomic accelerator that many of you already know as the Ascension chair used on the inner planes for several purposes. There are many of you who have studied the teachings of the former dispensations with Saint Germain, where this concept has been mentioned several times, but may not be fully understood. Allow us to give you now a greater understanding of this wondrous tool, beloved ones, so that you can use it to assist yourselves and others on your pathway to Ascension.

As I speak, the energy of Master Saint Germain is here with me, and it is both of us collectively now speaking to you, unifying our energies as one. In the light realms, there is such a unity of consciousness that we can blend our energies and thoughts easily; we enjoy this very much.

The atomic accelerator, or the Ascension chair, is a gift to the Earth and to humanity from the heart of beloved Master Saint Germain. It is a tool to assist the raising of vibration of a candidate for Ascension. It contains the frequencies of the pure white Light of the Ascension Flame. It can also be used to raise one's vibration gradually and gently. When the dial is turned on full force, it will literally lift someone into the vibration of the electronic body for full, instant and permanent Ascension into the light realm, and fifth dimensional consciousness.

In the past and now, many candidates on the inner planes, when ready for their earthly graduation, have received their full and majestic Ascension ceremony in the Light Realm, honored and supported by a large gathering of masters and beings from many dimensions, by sitting on one of these chairs. When the button is turned on full force, all energies remaining in the records of the candidate less than pure Light and pure Love are dissolved in the intensity of the Ascension frequency. The candidate is instantly transformed and reconnected with the fullness of their Divine Essence, with all spiritual gifts and attributes restored.

This is the true and permanent ceremony of divine union, beloveds! This is the great alchemical marriage with Self that so many of you are longing for. Although this is not the only way one can make their Ascension—there are indeed several other options—this is the one most commonly used now.

In order for one to receive this gift, one must definitely be spiritually ready at all levels, or the results could be disastrous. You can trust that none of us would ever offer to do this with anyone who has not yet attained the full level of initiations required to receive such a blessing. There are a few of these chairs on this planet kept in various spiritual, fifth dimensional retreats of the Great White Brotherhood. We have one in Telos and Saint Germain has one at his retreat at Jackson Peak in Wyoming. There is also one in the Himalayas and in a few other retreats.

Our channel, Aurelia, was directed by us several years ago to invite friends to her home once a month, to conduct a ritual Ascension ceremony for those desiring to deepen their commitment to this goal, to the spiritual hierarchy of this planet and to their I AM Presence. Each time Aurelia facilitated this ceremony with a group, a great number of us came to assist. Master Saint Germain always came with his portable atomic accelerator, which consists of a small etheric box which he positions under the chair in your dimension designed for that purpose.

Each time, Saint Germain himself controls the intensity and velocity that each candidate can receive in order to raise their vibration to the next level, without significant discomfort or disturbance of the present level. This moveable accelerator box is the same technology as a full version atomic accelerator chair in the light realm. But it is designed to be used for ceremonies performed in locations where surface people have chosen to do their Ascension work.

Aurelia has conducted these Ascension ceremonies since 1994, in her home while living in Montana. She has continued this service for the planet and for humanity ever since on a regular basis. She has performed this service of Light with every group that has come to Mount Shasta for initiatic journeys, and also in several other countries of the world during her travels abroad for conferences and workshops.

The Benefits and the Power of Building Momentum

We have noticed how wondrously powerful and beautiful the energies have become over the years, with each ritual Aurelia has facilitated adding energy to the sum total of all past ceremonies. With great interest and gratitude, we observed that after many years of regular practice of this ritual, the Chalice of Light now created with each ceremony is building a huge momentum. The energies almost double in intensity and beauty each time this sacred ceremony is performed. It affects and helps not only the people participating in the group, but creates a web of Light touching almost the entire planet.

Many of you are not making the progress on your spiritual journey as rapidly as you would like or achieving the results you want in your mundane endeavors. This is mainly because you are not in the habit of creating enough momentum to achieve your goals. Building greater momentum is needed to gather enough energy in your world to create whatever you want.

> *Even the beings portraying the "shadow side" understand this principle very well, and they are far more vigilant in building their momentum of darkness than the People of Light have been in building their momentum of Light.*

Your complacency is one of the main factors for the deep level of darkness, density and pain this whole planet has fallen into. Momentum of Light is what all those of us who have become masters have accumulated enough of in order to manifest whatever we want, at any time we desire it.

At first, in 1994, when Aurelia began to do her little ceremonies with four or five people, the Chalice of Light created with each ceremony was very small and not nearly as powerful as it is today. She continued to build her momentum, year by year, doing ceremonies each time she had enough people interested. She was unaware of its expanding impact.

With each ceremony, Master Saint Germain arrives with his etheric atomic accelerator box, invisible to those not yet clairvoyant, and puts it beneath the chair designated and decorated for that purpose. In our realm, we consider it to be a physical box, made of fifth dimensional technology and certain types of crystals. It has dials that one can turn on and off, just like the technologies in your realm.

When the group is ready, and the invocation of intention is made by Aurelia, Master Saint Germain turns on the atomic accelerator. What does it do? All around and beneath the chair, there is an emanation of Ascension frequency that begins radiating outward. The person sitting on the chair receives according to his level of evolution and capacity to receive.

The process is monitored carefully because the Ascension Flame energy emanating from the little box could literally make you become invisible quickly if turned on full blast. Be assured that until the time for the full glory of your Ascension is offered, you will receive safe increments each time these ceremonies are performed.

As you evolve your consciousness, the Ascension Flame helps your purification process in greater measure each time, and assists in the raising of your vibration every time you set up your intention through this sacred ritual.

It is so beautiful when you do this, if you could only see it from our perspective. As you gather together, you assist and hold the energy for each other. Each person comes forth to sit on the chair to declare their intention vocally before their friends and before their God to express their desire and intention for Ascension. The candidate also declares the willingness to do whatever it takes to make this happen. As the candidate formulates a prayer, Master Saint Germain adjusts the dial of his accelerator to flood the forcefield with the level of Ascension frequency appropriate for that person in the now moment.

Each time you speak from the heart on the chair and set your intention, you create an explosion of Love and Light that is most wondrous to behold. This is why, when you hold these gatherings, there is always a large assembly of Light Beings from the many realms of this planet, many other planets and star systems who delight in seeing what you are doing. They wish to witness this wondrous explosion of Light created by members of surface humanity. They always add to your momentum of Light their love, support and comfort.

How to Create Your Ceremony

What you do is to gather in a circle. Each person comes forth to sit on the designated Ascension Chair and states their intention, preferably aloud with a fully opened heart, their goals for this life and their Ascension. Make the most honorable prayer your heart dictates or inspires you to do at this moment.

Each person holds in her/his hands a special crystal provided by the facilitator, and sits on the chair for about three to five minutes. When finished, he/she gives a sign of completion with the eyes, and the group sings three "AUMs" to assist anchoring this energy in the physical while the person remains seated. Prior to singing each AUM, the facilitator or designated person, rings the Tibetan bells once. Then the person returns to his/her seat, and the next person comes forth. People do not need to come in a specific order. There is always a natural flow created and each one takes his/her turn when they feel ready. The facilitator usually goes last, but this is not a rule.

When everyone is finished, Saint Germain, Serapis Bey and myself, Adama, invite you to drink an elixir which we charge with the frequency of the "Golden Liquid Light." The facilitator pours sparkling apple juice or some other juice into small containers and distributes it to the group.

The facilitator, or someone else, makes a short invocation to ask that the liquid each person holds in their right hand be infused with the frequency of the Golden Liquid Light. The one making the invocation pauses for a moment for the officiating masters to transform the liquid at the frequency that is most appropriate for each person. When given the signal, each person slowly drinks the liquid that has now become a sacred alchemical elixir, expressing their deep gratitude for the gift and the rich blessings that are bestowed upon them.

The elixirs created during Ascension activations are just as effective as the ones we give you on the inner plane. You heard or read in one of the I AM books, around 1930, when David Lloyd drank the elixir given to him by Saint Germain on Mount Shasta, he immediately began to disappear and ascended into the Realms of Light in front of a crowd, creating much wonderment for each one present. Know, beloved ones, that David LLoyd could have made his Ascension differently, but it was the choice he made in the inner plane to ascend in this special manner, and it was granted. It happened this way for him because it was his time to ascend.

We could also charge the elixir for you in such a way that you could disappear, but that's not the plan for you right now. We are simply not going to do that, even if you ask! Not until it is your time, and believe us, several people have made that

The Fourth Ray

request. Sorry friends, for those who have requested this, but it is imperative that you wait for your right timing.

There will come a time in the future when group Ascension will manifest, and in some cases, it will happen in front of others who will witness this. This time is not so far away. This will never take anyone who ascends by surprise. If this happens to you, it is because you are totally prepared and have fully consented to this type of Ascension.

When you hold your gatherings with the atomic accelerator, Master Saint Germain always controls the exact amount of energy given to each one, according to the level of vibration each person can handle.

Some of you are hesitant or shy to speak your heart openly in front of your brothers and sisters. Know, dear ones, in the light realms there are no secrets; everything is known. It is best that you start getting used to it now if you intend to come here. It will be easier later. Once you make it to the higher dimensions nothing can be hidden. It is a very good practice to be able to open your heart in front of your brothers and sisters and hold nothing back.

There is no shame in what you are doing! It is so beautiful! It creates an explosion of Light each time, and your Light is amplified as you support each other, building a Momentum of Light on your "journey to the stars."

We invite you now to start meeting in groups of all sizes in your cities, villages and countries, at least once a month, as brothers and sisters, to reinforce your desires and intentions for your spiritual goals. Allow a momentum to build with each ceremony and with each one's intentions.

Imagine how powerful this can be! What you will be doing is creating little webs of Ascension Light everywhere on the planet that will gain greater and greater momentum as more and more people do this. This Momentum of Light will gain greater power as the energies created join together. This is the great Momentum of Light and Ascension Flame that is needed to propel this planet and all of humanity choosing to ascend in a great swirling tornado of Ascension Light that will dissolve all darkness on this planet, fully restoring back every man, woman and child to the dignity of their divinity.

This is how darkness will be totally dispelled and swallowed up in a great victory of Light. But you have to do your part in your dimension, beloved children of our heart. It will not simply happen automatically without your contribution and participation, or by wishing it to be so.

We from Telos enjoy very much your ceremonies of Love and Intention. Be assured that I, Adama, Lord Serapis Bey and Master Saint Germain shall be with you every time you perform your ceremonies, supporting and loving you all the way to your own victorious Ascension day.

Adama - Do you want to comment or do you have any questions on this subject?

Aurelia - This is the most incredible offering that you have given us about getting groups together around the world, and experiencing levels of Ascension frequency through facilitating Ascension ceremonies and taking in spiritual elixirs. You are offering us a permanent increase of frequency through this beautiful ritual, is that correct?

Adama - We are, and you can do it as often as you wish. It is up to you if you want to use this as a tool to assist yourself on your pathway. It is a tool whose energies simply build up and increase as you unite together. Many people want to ascend, but they often forget to set their intention and are not always willing to put in the effort necessary to attain the fullness of their spiritual freedom.

In the time of Lemuria, we used to participate in Ascension ceremonies weekly. Even the children participated with other children of their age group and enjoyed this very much. In fact, for most children, the permission to attend those ceremonies was considered a reward they looked forward to each week.

When you get together and reinforce your intentions, it becomes more powerful in your life. These gatherings can be created as wonderful ways to spend time together with likeminded people. You can even share a meal together afterwards, if you wish. This is the Lemurian way, to do things together very simply, without pomp or circumstance, simply being the gods and goddesses that we are. We invite you to do and be the same. Take advantage of these tools that help you raise your consciousness in very simple and pleasant ways.

And so be it, beloved children of our heart. Be in peace and in love with yourself. Soon, we will meet you face to face in the arms of Love.

The Seven Sacred Flames

Master Hilarion

Chapter Five

The Fifth Ray:

The Flame of Healing and Manifestation

Main God qualities and actions of the Fifth Ray:
Healing at all levels, truth, constancy, creation through manifestation, God's abundance through the immaculate heart of Mary.

Corresponding Chakra: Third Eye
Color: Green
Corresponding Stones: Emerald, Jade, Chrysoprase, Ruby Zozyte

Chohan of the Fifth Ray:
Master Hilarion
His Retreat: The Temple of Truth, Crete, Greece

Archangels of the Fifth Ray with Divine Complement:
Raphael and Mother Mary
Their Retreat: Temple of Healing, Fatima, Portugal

Elohim of the Fifth Ray with Divine Complement:
Cyclopea and Virginia
Their Retreat: Altain Range, China

About Master Hilarion, A True Master of the Healing Arts

Master Hilarion comes with wonderful energy and embodies pure, unconditional love. He is ever ready to assist us in our growth and goal of returning from whence we came. One of his primary focuses is that of Healing, reaching out to all who desire his assistance. His healing is all-encompassing and includes the healing of the physical body, as well as the healing of emotions, the mind and Spirit. He is also a teacher of Truth and Science. Hilarion and his Brotherhood are the self-appointed guardians of those blessed children of Earth who have devoted their lives to further the cause of Science, the secrets of Nature and the alchemy of the Fifth Ray.

Embodiments of Master Hilarion

- Hilarion was the high priest of the Temple of Truth on Atlantis and he transported the Flame of Truth to Greece a short time before the sinking of the continent. The focus of truth he established became the focal point of the Oracle of Delphi, a place where the high initiates of that temple acted as messengers of God under the sponsorship of Pallas Athena for hundreds of years.

- Hilarion was embodied as Saul of Tarsus who later became the Apostle Paul in the time of the ministry of Jesus. He is known for his spiritual encounters with the Christ in that embodiment.

- As Saint Hilarion (290-371 AD), he was the founder of monasticism in Palestine. He spent twenty years in the desert in preparation for his mission before he performed his first miracle. Crowds would gather to be healed from disease and unknown spirits. His life was filled with miracles of healing for everyone who came to see him and he made his ascension in that life. His gifts of healing were very much those of an adept.

He built the reputation of a truly great healer, able to bring souls to a spiritual resolution and understanding of their problems. He was also able to heal with the touch of a hand or the command: "Be thou made whole." He walked in the shadow of his "I AM Presence," being humble before God and his fellowmen. He gave God the glory for the miracles of healing performed through him. At the conclusion of his work and wondrous life, Master Hilarion finally made his Ascension in 371 AD.

The Temple of Truth

In the etheric realm over the beautiful Island of Crete, surrounded by the blue waters of the Mediterranean Sea, you will find the Temple of Truth, focus of Master Hilarion, Chohan of the Fifth Ray and the Brotherhood of Truth, who serve with him in this particular branch of the Spiritual Hierarchy.

The temple is very much like the Grecian temples with many gracefully carved columns of large proportions. It looks like the beautiful Parthenon erected so long ago to the beloved Pallas Athena, the Goddess of Truth, who is the cosmic patroness of this Brotherhood. The brothers wear pure white robes. Within this retreat exists one of the most ancient school rooms of the planet dedicated to the training of students and disciples in the magnetizing of Universal energy. They also teach students scientific and mathematical precision by which suns, planets and individual atoms are created and sustained.

This Brotherhood is appointed as the guardian presence of those on Earth who devote their lives to furthering the cause of Science in the treatment of disease and imbalances, whatever form they take. If invited and welcomed, they also assist doctors, nurses and missionaries with their work.

The Temple of Truth plays host to the great spiritual teachers of many ages who left their imprint of love and service upon the Earth. This is the temple where the full momentum of Truth from the Heart of God is focused on Earth for distribution worldwide. Those who earnestly desire to know and understand "truth" become the students of the Brotherhood at Crete.

In that retreat, a great audience chamber has become the place where the Master Jesus, along with the ascended representatives of former great religions which have blessed mankind throughout the ages, are given the opportunity to teach many souls. They teach those who either no longer believe in God as such, or through disillusionment and bitter experiences with incompetent religious teachers in whom they had placed their trust, have experienced deceptions and betrayal. These have lost their faith and conviction in God and the Supreme Intelligence that governs the Universe. Jesus endeavors in that retreat to present these souls with the knowledge of "Universal Truths" to restore their faith, hope, trust and belief in their own divinity and the divinity of the Father/Mother God.

About Healing

Nearly all health problems, no matter what form they take or whatever name they have been given by the medical establishment, are caused by lack of harmony, imbalances and unresolved issues, past or present, in the emotional body. In order to heal the body you must first heal the deep-seated feelings that cause the disturbances. When harmony in the emotional body is restored, the body will align easily and the healing you seek will become permanent.

The Fifth Ray

When you wish to heal yourself or assist others, it is important that you first connect with your own "I AM Presence" and your "Higher Mental Body," and the "I AM Presence" of the person you wish to assist. Express love and gratitude for your and their existence and the lessons life's experience is teaching you both. Then call upon the Law of Forgiveness for any transgressions of the Law of Love and for the neglect that has been displayed towards your Divine Essence.

Commune deeply with your Divine Source, the Governor of your lifestream that is always waiting for your recognition to assist you. Speak to it as you would to your very closest friend. Pour your love into all your bodies and thank your body elemental for its assistance. Call on the Law of Forgiveness for whatever has been the cause and core of your inharmony and call upon the transmutation powers of the Violet Flame with great love, intensity and gratitude.

For healing assistance, visualize the luminous presence of Jesus/Sananda, Master Hilarion, Mother Mary, or other Ascended Masters blazing white light or the color required in your auric field. For energy, use the color blue; for love and comfort, use pink; for peace, use gold and pink; for illumination, use yellow; and for healing, use emerald green, pink or violet. Although the main color for healing is green, all colors and all flames have wondrous healing properties.

Four Lady Masters govern the healing activities on Earth. They are Mary, the mother of Jesus/Sananda, Nada, the beloved twin flame of Jesus/Sananda, Meta, the daughter of Sanat Kumara and Kuan Yin, the Goddess of Compassion.

The Body Elemental

Everyone in human form has at its service a "body elemental" of great intelligence which animates and controls the mechanism of their physical body. From time to time, it becomes antagonistic toward the form it is assigned to when there is abuse and no love for the body or gratitude towards the body elemental for the dedicated and faithful service it renders. The body elemental is often required to serve the energy of the same lifestream from the time of the first embodiment upon planet Earth until the soul attains Ascension.

This body elemental has often been compelled by the Lords of Karma to activate and maintain the physical body it has been assigned to each time the soul takes a new incarnation. It is the body elemental that assists the beating of your heart, activates your nervous system and takes care of the proper functions of the organs and all systems. It can be reprimanded when any portion of the physical body ceases to function properly.

The truth is that because of the misuse of free will and the lack of mastery and love over the uncontrolled emotional, mental, etheric and physical bodies of the soul, these energies create chaos in the physical body. The body elemental is then forced to work very hard to repair such repetitive damage, without ever receiving recognition or gratitude from the soul it serves so faithfully. The same as you like to receive recognition and gratitude for services that you render to other human beings, it is important that you acknowledge your body elemental daily, sending it waves of Love, Golden Light and endless Gratitude. This attitude creates an affinity between you, the body elemental and your physical form for more harmony and better health. The hierarchs of the body elementals are the Elohim Hercules and Amazonia of the First Ray of God's Will.

Your body elemental is approximately three to four feet tall, and takes on your look with the perfections and imperfections you have created. It often dress like you. It often stands on your shoulder and those who are able to see elementals often see the body elemental of each person. Your body elemental is longing to outpicture divine perfection in your body again.

Before the fall in consciousness, the body elemental of each human did not know imperfection and was trained to maintain your body in perfect health, beauty and elegance. With the misuse of free will and the creation of karma, the body elemental was forced to integrate into the physical body the energies of the karmic debts you have incurred through lack of love, self hatred, violence and negligence in thoughts, actions and feelings. We ask you, beloveds, to express much gratitude, deep love and compassion for your body elemental. Your body elemental will also make its ascension with you and truly desires to assist you fully in this process. This means it will graduate to a higher level of service, which all body elementals desire for their evolution.

Transmission from the Beloved Hilarion
Master of Healing, Truth and Science

It is with much joy and eagerness that I bring the blessings and love of the Temple of Truth to all those who will connect with and study this material. The Brotherhood of Crete also joins me to amplify the energies and thought forms being created as you read and open your heart to receive the "truths" contained and expressed herein. Perceive them as opportunities for transformation and tools for enlightenment. Thank you Aurelia for giving me the opportunity to express myself in your writings!

We have been observing humanity for a very long time, and now we observe carefully how our teachings are received by each one coming in contact with them and what each of you do with these "Pearls of Wisdom and Knowledge." So much teaching has been given to humanity in the past in various forms and through various channels, and so little has been fully understood, used and integrated.

Many of you are ever so interested in the next teaching or the next transmission of Light offered and so on. Some of you read one book after the other, but your consciousness does not attain the level of spiritual learning it was meant to arouse within you. As soon as you receive one or several of these pearls you feel temporarily exalted; but you quickly put it aside to attend the next occupation or read the next book. You more often than not forget the wisdom that has come your way within less than an hour or a day.

For many, but not all, you go on about your life without ever allowing your consciousness to stay still or contemplate long enough what you have just read or heard to integrate the full blessing and transformation of consciousness that any true teaching of Light is meant to create. In fact, any true teaching that you receive or read about, if received lightly and not contemplated from the perspective of the heart, and not allowed to literally create the miracles of Love it is meant to generate within you, becomes clutter in your mind instead of a blessing.

For example, if you read this material only once for curiosity's sake, without absorbing and integrating the "Pearls of Truth and Wisdom" it contains to advance the evolution of your consciousness, you will not gain from your investment the deep impact and gifts presented to you. Our teachings are not comic books, dear ones; they are not meant to simply entertain you for a moment. The teachings of the Ascended Masters contain cosmic truths meant to pull you out of the spiritual slumber you have been in for thousands of years. They are meant to assist you in the restoration of the consciousness of your divinity and the restoration of all the spiritual gifts lying dormant within the deep recesses of your hearts which you have allowed to dwindle to almost nothing. They are meant to assist you forge enough spiritual mastery to make of you "ascended beings," able to join the rank of the immortals with all the benefits that come with it. They are meant to assist you reach all the goals for your incarnation.

As Saint Hilarion, I did not have much human education and I did not receive any direct teachings of truth from my guides and masters as you have been so privileged to receive in the last century, particularly in the last two decades, in such abundance. A great part of my life was spent as a hermit in the desert, seeking daily, and moment-to-moment, with an intense burning desire in my heart to reconnect and externalize the God within, that wondrous Flame of Love that is the I AM Presence living within the Sacred Heart of each soul.

I invested over 20 years contemplating the qualities of that Sacred Heart and becoming it before my gifts returned to me. And when they externalized, it was because I had invested much time in contemplating my true nature as a divine being that I had embodied the great momentum of my Divine Essence. Then the God within allowed me to use my new found mastery and gifts to heal all those who came to me the rest of that incarnation. And believe me, they came by the thousands. I made my glorious ascension in the Light from that lifetime, soon after my transition to the other side of the veil.

I chose to leave all worldly pursuits in that life to seek the "only one" of true value to me. My devotion, my determination, my constancy and my unwavering faith that I would attain the goal of my incarnation bore the fruit of my quest and changed the course of my evolution forever. I was offered my Ascension at the conclusion of that life, and sometime after, I was offered the privilege of holding the Office of the Chohan of the Flame of Healing for the planet.

This is the precious message I want to convey to all of you today, that to become a "Master of Light" and free yourself from all your human shackles and limitations requires investment in Self. Once you have found the teachings or the books that give you the inspiration and the tools to make your Ascension, you no longer need to shop for more. You need to get busy applying the wisdom from the material and information you already have and forge your mastery with it.

Come to us in the retreats during your sleep time. I promise that you will be well received; it will be our great pleasure to teach you and to coach you in the areas you have alignments to make or weaknesses to conquer. We will be happy to become part of your support team on your evolutionary pathway. We have vast pools of knowledge and truth on various subjects of interest, especially on healing and science, that we would like to share with you. Those who come are most fascinated with the information and wisdom they can acquire by frequenting our retreat.

All of the Chohans of the Rays and the Brotherhoods of Light work very closely with Adama and the Lemurian Brotherhood of Telos. In fact, at inner levels, they have been guides and helpers of humanity for a long time. Before many of us made our Ascension, it was the Lemurians of Telos who were our closest and most dedicated guides and spiritual mentors. Now we have joined their teams and we all work together for the wondrous and noble cause of uplifting humanity into its Ascension in the Light along with Mother Earth. Together, we are dedicated and determined to manifest the return of Life on the surface of the planet as it was during the former Great Golden Ages.

The Fifth Ray

I am Hilarion, Chohan of the Fifth Ray, holding my cup of Love and Healing to you. Will you accept it? Will you prepare your heart and consciousness, diligently and with constancy, to discover the God-within, the greatness of who you are and the wonders that are awaiting you if you apply yourself to attain what we have attained? Are you willing to do whatever it will take to make it happen?

The Seven Sacred Flames

Third Eye Chakra

The Fifth Ray

Prayer for Fifth Ray Healing

Invocation to the Flame of Healing

Beloved I AM Presence, Beloved Angels of the Healing Flame, Beloved Mother Mary and Archangel Raphael, beloved Hilarion and all Beings of Light serving on the Ray of Healing.

I come now before Thy flame to request healing in God's name. I stand with my God Presence to be liberated and healed from all physical burdens through Thy Healing Light and Love. I also ask to be healed from all etheric scars, mental and emotional traumas from this life and from the past.

Flame of Healing of purest green,
bless my form and make me whole!
Pour comfort into my soul and enlightenment for my mind.
I AM God's Perfection manifest in body, mind and soul.
I AM God's Healing Light flowing to make me whole.
I AM the Master Presence charging all my bodies with Love.
Beloved God Presence, as I transform my consciousness,
Let heaven's perfection manifest in my daily life,
Send thy Ray of Healing upon my soul!

I AM Christ Presence charging me with Thy Radiant Healing Light until I become the full manifestation of that Light. Beloved I AM! Beloved I AM! Beloved I AM!

Discourse from Adama with Master Hilarion

Adama speaks to us about healing and Lemuria. A profound meditation takes us to the Great Jade Temple of Telos, where what we experience is incredibly healing and refreshing.

Greetings, my friends, this is Adama of Telos. Whenever we are invited for contact and to give our teachings, it is always a moment of joy and fulfillment for us. Today, we would like to discuss a new approach to healing, and bring to you an awareness of a wonderful healing temple that we have in Telos, the Great Jade Temple. The access to this awesome temple has been closed to surface dwellers since the demise of our continent.

Recently, however, the doors of this great healing temple have been re-opened to all who wish to visit. You are invited to come here in your etheric bodies to recharge, to purify and to learn about healing with a new level of understanding. This new dispensation is indeed a privilege that all of you on the surface can take advantage of during this time of great change and healing for humanity and for the planet.

The Great Jade Temple was physical in the time of Lemuria, and its main focus has been "healing" in the true sense of the word. This temple was first erected in the time of Lemuria, and for hundreds of thousands of years its energies blessed the lives of the people. Inside the temple burned the immortal, unfed flame of healing for the planet. The immortal flame was nurtured by the angelic kingdom, by the Holy Spirit and also by the love of the people of Lemuria. The energies of this temple held the balance of true healing for the planet itself, for her inhabitants and for your Earth Mother.

When we realized that our continent was in danger and would eventually be destroyed, we also knew that this majestic temple would be lost in its physical expression. We endeavored to build its physical replica in Telos. Although the replica is smaller than the original temple, all the records of the energies of the "Immortal Flame of Healing" since the time of its creation were transferred to Telos for safekeeping. It is still gathering momentum to this day. This awesome healing energy was never lost to the planet, even with the destruction of our continent. All of its energies and treasures were moved prior to Lemuria's demise.

The planning for the building of the replica of this temple and the moving of its energies took place 500 years before Lemuria went down. Many other replicas of important temples were also built in Telos in the same manner. In order to save our culture, and as many of our people as possible, we had to plan our strategy 5,000 years ahead of the actual time of the foreseen cataclysms.

Healing is so greatly needed at this time for all of you, and this is why we have opened the doors of the Great Jade Temple to assist humanity now.

It is our joy to invite you to come here in your etheric body at night, and to receive a much greater understanding of true healing than the one you presently hold. When you come here, we have as guides a great number of our people who are always willing to take you "under their wings" spiritually, to assist you with your healing of the deep traumas and sorrows of the past and the present. As you heal your inner pain and traumas, you will also heal the difficult conditions in your lives and your physical bodies.

External pains and difficulties are always the mirrors of inner pains and fears. They mirror to you what needs to be healed and transformed in your consciousness. We can assign three counselors for each of you who come here; they can assist you with whatever is most needed for your return to wholeness. One counselor focuses with you on your emotional body, another focuses with you on your mental body and a third one focuses on the healing of your physical body, all in total harmony and synchronicity. In this way, your healing becomes a more balanced project than if you just focus on one aspect of yourself, without understanding and transforming your internal programming. You know, when one aspect of yourself is not in perfect balance, it affects all other aspects of your being.

And how does one get to the Great Jade Temple in his or her etheric body?

By intention, my friend! What you need to do is to set your intention to come to this temple in your meditation or before you go to sleep at night. As an example, you may say, to your GodSelf and your guides and masters the following prayer. *"From the Lord God of my Being, I request to be taken to the Great Jade Temple in Telos this night. I now ask my guides, masters and angels to take me there as my body rests from the activities of the day."* You may also formulate your own prayer requests. Set your intention that you want to come here for recharging, for purification, for healing, for counseling, or simply to have communion and interaction with us.

We know how to take care of you once you get here. Basically, in your higher soul body you know how to get here yourself; simply trust that it is happening, even if you do not have any conscious recollection of your experience. It is not yet meant to be. Your etheric body looks almost identical to your physical body except it is more perfect. It feels as physical to you when you are here in your etheric body. This is what you are moving toward in your future. Your transformed body will also feel very physical to you, although it will be relieved of much density and the frequency will be vibrating at a much higher level.

In the process of transforming your consciousness and your physical body, you are not losing anything. You are integrating higher, more subtle vibrations and higher light. All you will be losing is unwanted density. Your body will become more refined, more beautiful, limitless, immortal and it will feel just as physical as it does now, except you won't have to experience limitation of any kind. You will travel with the speed of thought and it is going to be a lot of fun, I promise!

***What are some requests that one could bring
to the temple for healing that are most appropriate?***

Basically on the planet most people have physical problems of some sort, and a lot of hidden fears which trigger many challenges in your daily life. You have emotions trapped in your subconscious and unconscious mind that were imprinted on your soul from many past experiences that were not simply painful, but often very traumatic. These experiences were the lessons needed for your evolutionary pathway.

Everyone has an accumulation of emotional trauma in their feeling body from many thousands of embodiments. What is needed now is resolution for final clearing, healing and the acquisition of greater wisdom for which these experiences were created. Any experience that was not cleared in a given lifetime keeps replaying the same programming again and again in all subsequent lifetimes until true healing, wisdom and understanding take place in the depth of the soul.

The sadness, the sorrow, the grief, every emotional trauma, and anything that you experience that does not reflect the natural pure joy, bliss and ecstasy of your being, indicate what needs healing within yourself. Conscious and subconscious fears hold you back and need to be cleared in everyone's consciousness. Mental toxins coming from lifetimes of embracing erroneous belief systems and distorted programming are now showing themselves to your awareness in one way or the other to be cleared and healed. Be aware and attentive to the promptings of your soul. A person may choose the most important issues for their healing in the moment and bring that issue to the temple for resolution.

Our guides will discuss with you the lessons and wisdom that need to be understood in your consciousness, and what steps you need to take to assist your manifestation of permanent and true healing. Your healing can be very much compared to the peeling of a huge onion with hundreds of layers, which you will heal one by one until completion. You then become a pure mirror of divinity, and all things will open to you, beyond your wildest dreams.

Much of this work, but not all, can be done at night while your body sleeps and can be integrated later in your daily life. You don't need to know what every fear and all past experiences are about. All you need to do is consciously release these energies, whatever their names. Our guides can give you much insight for your particular healing needs. In turn, you bring back this new wisdom within your subconscious, and you start applying it in your waking state. Your meditations with your Divine Presence will resurrect a greater awareness in your consciousness.

Your inner work is the most important step you want to take at this time to accelerate your evolution and to open the way for your homecoming.

Our counselors at the temple will give you, at the soul level, an expanded view of why you are experiencing certain health problems. They will show you why a certain difficulty persists in your life and how you have created it, whether it is physical, mental or emotional. With the assistance of our counselors,

The Fifth Ray

you will learn to heal yourself and all the pains and distortions imprinted in your soul. Before any complete and permanent physical healing can take place, the emotional causes or distortion in your belief systems have to be addressed and released. These are not band-aid solutions, but permanent healing.

Know that all physical problems, even if they appear to be accidents, always have their roots in the emotional and mental bodies. Mental stress and mental illnesses also have their roots in the emotions. The emotional body is the most important area to begin with for your healing. The traumas of the destruction of the continents of Lemuria and Atlantis, when people were separated from their loved ones and their families overnight, have given birth to much fear, sadness, sorrow and despair in the souls of humanity, and have been carried forward lifetime after lifetime.

It is now time to completely heal the past and embrace a brand new paradigm of love, limitlessness and unprecedented grace for your life and for the planet. In Telos, we are your brothers and sisters, close friends of the past who love you all so very much. It is our joy to extend to you all the assistance we are allowed at this time for the purpose of your complete transformation, resurrection and ascension into the realms of Love and Light.

You know, your heart is the great intelligence of your soul and is one with the Mind of God. It holds all memories of all aspects of you since the beginning, and it will never mislead you. Your heart is the part of your beingness that you can really learn to know and trust again. You have closed your hearts, beloved ones, because your pain and fears have been so great. Closure has been a form of protection for you in the past. It has served your evolution in wondrous ways that you will come to understand some day, but at this time, it no longer serves you.

Many of you are clinging to your old pain and fears simply because it has become fearful for you to open your hearts to unconditional love and let go of your old outmoded erroneous beliefs. You have a fear that if you open your hearts to life unconditionally, you will be inflicted with more pain. Your old fears and pain have become so familiar to you that you have found a level of security and comfort in them.

How do we actually open our hearts and allow our emotional bodies to begin the healing process?

There is no one recipe for everyone. Each one is unique and has different issues to heal. Each of you has a different emotional make-up and your own distinct healing process. Basically, you will start the process moving in the right direction through choice, sustained intention, conscious and active meditation, and diligent communication with your higher self each day. Ask the part of you that remains in divine wholeness to reveal to you what needs healing in the now moment, and to bring it forth to your conscious awareness.

Start signaling your I AM Presence with serious intention that you want to be whole again, and that you want to integrate all parts of yourself in unity and oneness. Submit yourself willingly to whatever process is necessary to receive that healing in full trust, faith, love and surrender. Be assured that you will receive the full cooperation of your higher self and the whole of the light realm. Your healing process will then begin to take place at every level.

Your higher self will draw to you the right books to read, the right people to meet with, and events and opportunities will come your way. If you open your mind and heart to your healing with sustained intention and diligence, the process will flow with grace and ease.

Your healing process will continue to progress as you remain focused in your intention. It may appear to be work at first, and without doubt, it is. See it as a journey back to the "sun" of your being and know that this process is loaded with rewards and fulfillments along the way. You are not alone in this journey. Your angels, guides, masters, as well as all of us in the New Lemuria, are accompanying you at every step. The entire spiritual hierarchy of this planet, your Earth Mother and the whole of the light realm are at your beck and call to assist your healing.

As you progress in your healing, your energy will come back. Your physical body will start letting go of the pains and traumas of the past and you will start rejuvenating. You will begin to feel yourself becoming more alive and vibrant. Humanity has been working with 5 to 10% of their full potential as divine beings. The rest of your being has been there all along in a state of slumber. Wake-up and heal yourselves, beloveds. As you open your hearts and let go of your pain, you will become increasingly more alive. The joy that you will feel will be amplified many times. Your mental faculties will open more and you will think "oh well, we're all becoming geniuses now and life is so joyous!" Open yourself to grace in a very conscious manner and allow yourself to receive those energies in all of your bodies on a daily basis.

Do we actually ever reach a point where the mirrors stop?

Yes, my friend. Every time you work these things out within yourself, you go deeper and deeper. You are peeling layers, and some of them are very deep. Everyone has their own unique type of layers to peel off, but generally speaking there are many of them to deal with. When you think you have worked things out and you start feeling better and you think this is finished, it comes back again to be healed on a deeper level.

This is why now, in this particular time of the last incarnation for many of you, it seems more endless than ever before. In this lifetime, everything comes together not only from one or two or six incarnations, but also from the totality of all of your incarnations on the Earth. Every little thing manifests now to be healed. It may seem worse now, but actually it is much less than before.

Does the toxicity we encounter in our daily lives impact the speed of our healing process?

Well yes, it adds to the burdens you already have. Let me explain! You have many types of bodies, what you call various subtle bodies. You also have four main body systems; the physical vehicle, the emotional body, the mental body and the etheric body. Each of these have a great number of sublevel bodies as well. At this time, we are only going to discuss the four main bodies that each represent 25% of your totality. They work together; when you suppress one you suppress the others. When you heal one, you bring relief to the others as well. When you ingest or inhale toxic chemical substances into your body, be aware that there are certain types of substances that are fairly easy to eliminate from the body, and others for which the body has no mechanism of elimination.

Twenty-first century chemicals and pollution have been so thoroughly incorporated into your food, water, and air supplies that the body has great difficulty eliminating them. The toxic levels within your body continue to build up. When the body was designed, these man-made toxic substances did not exist. They have a tendency to lodge themselves in the cells, and only the right application of homeopathic and vibrational remedies is able to eliminate them. Do what you can to ingest into your bodies only the purest type of water, the purest types of liquids and foods. When you do not feel emotionally balanced, your physical body does not feel well either. You cannot separate any part of yourself without affecting the whole.

What I realize is that we can never be whole until we awaken, and until we heal each one of those bodies.

You cannot become whole if you avoid healing any part of your energetic make-up. The true and permanent healing takes place when you create balance at all levels. There are people who are physically ill, let's say with cancer. They are going to spend, if they have a lot of money, a fortune in obtaining physical healing by the cut, burn and poison methods of the medical establishment. The emotional aspect which caused the cancer in the first place is never addressed. In fact, much more stress and trauma are added to the already overburdened emotional body. What kind of permanent healing can be expected from such a denial of a basic aspect of Self?

Billions of dollars are spent each year in the application of band-aid solutions. Some people may experience temporary remissions at times, yes, but what occurs is not a true and permanent healing. Even when short-term relief is experienced, if the soul has not learned the new wisdom from the illness, the true healing has not taken place.

If the person ends up dying from the cut, burn and poison methodology, the healing and the lessons were not learned and the root of the problems seated in the emotional body were ignored. Whatever the emotional cause of the cancer is in the first place, if not addressed in one lifetime, it will be repeated again and again in subsequent incarnations until the deeper understanding and wisdom are reached.

Your "I AM Presence" requires that you learn all of your lessons of wisdom and truth before you can access your total spiritual freedom and your return to wholeness. This is why you have had so many incarnations to acquire the wisdom needed.

Angels, and many other beings from the light realm working with humanity, also come here regularly for purification and recharging. They don't need any counseling from us. The Great Jade Temple serves as a means of decontamination for them, a setting in which to unload the discordant energies picked up from their contact with surface humanity.

Your GodSelf, who is omniscient, works at the level of creation. It works very closely with angels and ascended masters, with the star brothers, and in cooperation with us for your healing. We are never permitted to perform healings for you without the permission of your GodSelf. In all your efforts and steps to heal yourself, you must always include and reconnect with your "I AM Presence" and state your intentions for whatever it is you want to accomplish or heal. Sometimes, there are people who get angry with the ascended masters or angelic presences because they feel their prayer requests have not been answered according to their expectations. They go on denying the very source of their desires, closing their hearts to further assistance.

This kind of attitude, beloved ones, is common among humanity. Those engaging in such mind-sets deprive themselves of much assistance, grace and blessings for that given incarnation. What you do not realize is that no ascended master or angelic presence can go beyond the pathway of your soul. Your "I AM" knows exactly what you need to learn and accomplish to meet your set goals for this lifetime. Any angel or ascended master will always work in full cooperation with your Divine Self to assist your "greater plan" and ultimate destiny. While you are in the third dimension, you are veiled and do not see the full perspective of your incarnation.

The Fifth Ray

Your "I AM" is your governor, and your soul represents the sum total of all your experiences. Ascension is the process of unifying all of this into oneness; you become totally whole again. You become the personification of your Divine Self, manifesting the fullness of your divinity right here on Earth. The final stage of ascension is the most wonderful event that could ever happen in anyone's evolution. For so many lifetimes you have worked toward that one goal, and in this lifetime you can achieve it fully. You can become all that you ever wanted to be, because the doors of ascension are now wide open, like never before in millions of years.

This is your chance to say yes to this great opportunity and do it. Ascension doors close and open, according to various cycles of evolution. It may be a very long time before they open as wide again. If you want to gain your spiritual freedom in this life and to experience the alchemical marriage of your soul with your GodSelf through the process of your ascension, there is no better time to do it than now. You must consciously and intentionally choose it and want it more than anything else. You are not going to be forced into it.

You are offered at this time the greatest of all opportunities. There are only a few years left before the Earth's Ascension. "Will you take our hands to learn from us so that we can assist your homecoming? We are already home. Will you come and join us?"

Meditation

Journey to the Great Jade Temple
With Adama and Master Hilarion

The Great Jade Temple is a wondrous and sacred place where beings from all dimensions on this planet and beyond come for healing. Those of the light realms who are directly assisting humanity come to this temple to cleanse and recharge their energies. It is used by galactic beings as well. This "famous" temple is popular and well visited. It is constructed mainly of the purest concentration of jade.

I ask now that you center yourself in your heart; sit comfortably and relax; and begin to integrate and receive the healing energies. You are now invited to come with us on a journey in consciousness to Telos to experience the Great Jade Temple beneath Mount Shasta. You are traveling here in your etheric body. Continue to center in your heart and state your intention to your guides to take you to Telos in consciousness to the portal of the Great Jade Temple, and they will. All your guides are familiar with this place, and they know exactly how to take you there. There are many of us there, waiting to receive you.

Bring your body in a state of relaxation and breathe very deeply as you focus your intention to be taken to the Great Jade Temple. Now see yourself there in your consciousness. See yourself arriving at the portal of this large temple, a four-sided pyramid made of the purest and highest quality jade stones. The head priest, also guardian of this temple, greets you. The floor is tiled with jade and pure gold. Fountains of golden green luminescent lights shoot their essence about 30 feet in the air from several areas, creating a very mystical effect. Feel yourself there and look at whatever is shown to you. Feel the air that

The Fifth Ray

you are now breathing in the temple and feel the invigorating energy created by all the fountains of pure healing energy permeating the air everywhere. How refreshing and rejuvenating it is for your whole body! Though you are there in your etheric body, you will bring back some of that vibration to your physical body. That is why it is so important that you breathe in deeply, taking in as much as you can of that healing energy.

Flowers of all shapes, shades and colors, along with a large variety of emerald green plants, are growing in large jade boxes creating a most magical environment. Gaze upon this unique beauty and feel the sacredness of the surroundings. Allow yourself to feel purity of the energies of that environment. The Head Priest introduces each of you to a member of our community who will be your specific guide and assistant for your journey here.

As you enter the temple with your guide, you see a very large stone made of pure jade, oval-shaped, about 10 feet in diameter and 18 feet high. This stone is of the purest and highest healing vibration. On the top of the stone, you see a round gold and jade chalice. It has a flat base and sides about two feet high. It is hosting the emerald green unfed Flame of Healing that has been burning perpetually for millions of years to assist Earth's inhabitants.

Now feel this healing flame deeply in your soul, in your heart and in your emotional body. Yes, you can also take your emotional body there. This awesome flame burns perpetually and maintains a major healing energy matrix for the planet. This flame has consciousness, my friends. It is fed eternally by the love of the Holy Spirit, the angelic kingdom and our love. As you approach the Jade stone, you are invited by the Guardian of the Healing Flame to sit on a chair made of pure jade to contemplate what it is in your life that most needs healing. What are the changes in your consciousness that you are willing to make to bring about that healing?

While in meditation, you are receiving telepathic guidance and assistance from your guides, and this guidance is imprinted in your heart and soul. Now, we will pause for a moment and allow you to have this interaction with your guides and with your higher self for your healing. *(Pause)* See and feel the jewels, the crystals and healing energies of the temple and breathe them in. Breathe in this healing energy as deeply as you can; you are going to take this energy back into your physical body. Keep breathing it in. You are on the most sacred healing vibration site of the planet. Take as long as you need.

When you are done, get up from your chair and walk around the temple with your guide. Look at the beauty and the healing energies. Feel free to communicate to him/her the burdens of your heart and ask for further assistance for your healing. Be open to whatever is going to be revealed to you. If you don't remember your journey consciously, do not be concerned. For most of you are getting the information at some other level.

When you feel complete, come back to consciousness in your body and take several deep breaths. Know that you can return there any time you want. Each time, you will be assisted in the same manner. The more often you return, the more of a rapport you are creating with us.

We now conclude this meditation by sending you love, peace and healing. We are holding our hands out to you in assistance, love and guidance. We are only as far away as a thought and a whisper, or a request from your heart. And so be it!

Chapter Six

The Sixth Ray:

The Flame of Resurrection

Main God qualities and actions of the Sixth Ray:
Ministration of the love of Christ, selfless service of God and mankind, devotion to one's fellowmen, spiritual worship through devotion and reverent feelings.

Corresponding Chakra: Solar Plexus
Color: Purple and Gold
Corresponding Stones: Citrine, Pyrite, Golden Calcite

Chohans of the Sixth Ray:
Lord Sananda and Lady Nada *(known in their last incarnation as Jesus and Mary Magdalene).*
Their Retreats: The Temple of Resurrection near Jerusalem, a Retreat in Saudi Arabia, North East of the Red Sea, a place for gatherings where various councils of Light of the Great White Brotherhood often meet.

Archangels of the Sixth Ray with Divine Complement:
Uriel and Aurora
Their Retreat: Tatra Mountains, Poland

Elohim of the Sixth Ray with Divine Complement:
Peace and Aloha
Their Retreat: Hawaiian Islands

The Seven Sacred Flames

Lord Sananda

The Sixth Ray

Lady Nada, Goddess of Love

About Lady Nada and Lord Sananda

Formerly embodied in their last incarnation as Jesus and Mary Magdalene, Nada and Sananda both work together to assist the Earth and the evolution of humanity towards Ascension through the pathway of unconditional love on the Sixth Ray of service and ministration of the Love of Christ.

Ascended Lady Master Nada is Chohan of the Sixth Ray along with her beloved twin flame, Lord Sananda. Together, they embody the Purple and Gold Ray of peace, service, ministration, and true brotherhood. She holds the energy of Divine Love for humanity, along with Lord Sananda, and works very closely with him. She is also known as the Goddess of love.

Lady Nada oversees a retreat, which is situated in the etheric realms above Lake Titicaca at the border of Bolivia and Peru. Ascended Masters Mary *(known as Mother Mary)*, Kuan Yin, Pallas Athena, Lady Venus and Lady Portia *(Saint Germain's twin flame)* are all working closely together in that retreat. From this place in Bolivia, they distribute powerful feminine energies to our planet in order to balance the distortions still existing between the masculine and feminine energies. There is a strong emphasis at present time on restoring the balance between the female and male polarities within ourselves, within our relationships and in the world.

Many of these female Masters are working to help us with this task so vitally imperative for the Ascension of humanity. Unless humanity begins manifesting more balance between the masculine and feminine expressions of power in the world, we will not easily experience the changes in consciousness which must take place before the period 2010-2012. The long awaited Golden Age can only manifest when divine balance between the male and female polarities becomes a reality on the planet.

Lady Nada tutors candidates for Ascension in mastering the God qualities of the solar-plexus chakra and preparing to receive the gifts of the Holy Spirit. Nada is also a messenger for Lord and Goddess Meru, the Manus of the fourth root race, whose retreat and Temple of Illumination is situated at Lake Titicaca, South America.

Lady Nada has a certain cosmic authority for the incoming age; healing is one of her services to mankind, as well as the use of the Pink Flame. Her symbol is a pink rose. Nada is also a member of the Karmic Board, a group of eight ascended masters and cosmic beings who dispense justice to this system of worlds, adjudicating karma and mercy on behalf of every soul.

Through both these offices in the Great White Brotherhood *(Chohan of the Sixth Ray and member of the Karmic Board)*, Nada teaches the path of personal Christhood by expressing love through ministration and service to life. She assists ministers, missionaries, healers, teachers, psychologists and counselors of the law. She represents the Third Ray in her position with the Karmic Board. Lady Master Nada's etheric retreat is located over Saudi Arabia where she works with her beloved, Lord Sananda.

Lord Sananda
The Initiator of the Christian Dispensation

Lord Sananda represents Divine Love and the Higher Realms of Spirit. He is the symbol of Christianity for the Christian dispensation. He represents the Ascension process of Humanity rising back to the Godhead. In his primary role, he holds the office of "World Teacher" along with master Kuthumi. Master Jesus/Sananda has the task of purifying the distorted teachings initiated by the fears of the early fathers of the Christian churches and removing the man-made dogmas and doctrines which have corrupted the purity of His teachings, almost from the beginning, 2,000 years ago.

Regardless of your religion, you may call upon Lord Sananda to assist you in any area of your life. He is still forever present in consciousness with all of us personally and collectively. As the Hierarch of the Piscean Dispensation of the past 2,000 years, he now works closely with Master Saint Germain, the Hierarch of the Aquarian Age of the coming 2,000 years. Together, they form a great team sharing the same goals.

Whether you believe that Jesus/Sananda is the only Son of God, or whether you consider him an Ascended Master who came to Earth as a World Teacher and Healer, you may call upon Him for assistance. Indeed, he came to Earth to create a new philosophy that will eventually unite mankind with the Source of their Divinity. During his life as Yeshua Ben Joseph *(Jesus)*, he did not advocate any new religion, only living from the Heart and embracing one's own divinity.

Unfortunately, the Christian churches have distorted most of His original intention to teach us the simple ways of embracing one's own Christhood. Lord Sananda intended that God's Love and Wisdom be taught in a way that would be comprehensible for all to understand and integrate. His teachings were meant for everyone, not just for those who considered themselves more educated and appointed themselves as authorities, desiring to control and deceive humanity with false doctrines.

Lord Sananda is now more active than ever in teaching humanity the true concepts of the Christ consciousness which is manifested in its full splendor in Telos and all Cities of Light. It is time to seriously question the outdated teachings of Christian churches and seek the real Truth. It is certainly not the greatest soul wisdom to rely uniquely for "one's salvation" on the old, outmoded versions of spirituality taught by the early Christian churches which are, to say the least, incomplete. We must now understand and apply in our daily lives the true teachings given to us by former world teachers who came to assist humanity evolve their consciousness to the level of their Christhood.

Sananda works very closely with the Lemurian Brotherhood of Light of Telos, with Adama and the spiritual planetary hierarchy to resurrect the true teachings of the Christ consciousness initiated by him 2,000 years ago.

Embodiments of Lord Sananda

Sananda told me that he had many incarnations on the continent of Lemuria, but He was not specific. This great master had numerous embodiments on this planet before his last incarnation as Yeshua Ben Joseph, listed below.

- King David of the Old Testament. In that life, he worked closely with the prophet Samuel, who is one of the incarnations of our beloved Saint Germain.

- Joseph of Egypt, son of Jacob in the Old Testament, has some of the most interesting parallels to the life of Jesus. In Judaism, the Messiah was thought of as the son of Joseph as well as the son of David.

- Joshua, the one who led the Israelites into the Promised Land in the Old Testament.

- In his last incarnation, he embodied as Jesus. His real name was Yeshua Ben Joseph. This great master came to teach us that we have the power to create, heal and become the Christ as he demonstrated. He said, "These and greater things than these shall you do." (John 14:12) He demonstrated the power of God through His healings, His crucifixion and His resurrection. In that life, he was overshadowed by Lord Maitreya, the planetary Christ, whom he called "His Father," and indeed Maitreya was his spiritual "Father" and the great sponsor of his noble mission.

Embodiments of Lady Nada

- On Atlantis, Nada served as a priestess in the Temple of Love. The Sisterhood of that temple directed healing through love by the use of light rays for those who required and could receive them anywhere on Earth. That temple was patterned after a rose, each petal being a room. It still remains in the ethers, even to this day.

- Lady Nada was also a high priestess in the Temples of Isis and received her training in full mastery over several prior embodiments from that highly evolved "mystery school." These mystery schools no longer exist today; they will likely be restored in the new energy after the Ascension of the Earth into the fifth dimension.

- As Mary Magdalene, she incarnated with her beloved twin flame, Jesus, in his mission as the "embodiment of the Christ." She came to be his beloved companion to fully support his mission. Sananda told me that the account in the bible of the wedding at Cana is the true story of his official marriage to Mary Magdalene.

It is extremely important for this Truth to be revealed now, that Mary Magdalene was a high initiate and priestess of the Sacred Fire during her lifetime with Jesus. She had a very high degree of evolutionary attainment. Along with Mother Mary, she was with Him to hold the energies of the

Divine Feminine on his behalf during his ministry in the land of Galilee and at his crucifixion. She was certainly NOT the "sinner and prostitute" as depicted by scholars of the early churches. This denial of the divine feminine is one of the greatest lies that has been unjustly imposed and imprinted on humanity's consciousness for the last 2,000 years.

She was unfairly discriminated against by the early "fathers of the church" in their attempt to subdue, once more, the energies of the divine feminine for generations to come. They sought to maintain control over what they feared the most, the energies of "Divine Mother," that Mary Magdalene represented at that time, along with Mother Mary, the mother of Jesus. Both were very high initiates of the Temples of Isis and had the required attainment to hold that energy while Jesus was performing his Sacred Mission. It is time for humanity to open their hearts to the loving energies of Mary Magdalene, seeing her for who she really is and forgetting the lies maliciously invented against her.

Retreats of the Masters of the Sixth Ray

In the Far East, shining in the pulsating ethers over the Holy Land, stands the Temple of Resurrection, whose immortal flame of restoration and resuscitation is guarded and protected by the beautiful Ascended Masters Lords Sananda, Lady Nada and Mother Mary.

This temple is created of substance which resembles "mother of pearl." It is circular in design. The courts, like great cylinder corridors, circle around the Central Flame Room, where the heart of the Sacred Fire of Resurrection is focused. It is composed of seven circular corridors around the central altar where the unfed Flame of Resurrection burns perpetually, radiating its buoyant, uplifting, and life-giving resuscitating power. Beautiful beings from the Brotherhood of the Flame of Resurrection amplify its power in each one of the corridors.

Visitors to the Resurrection Temple enter the corridors where the radiation of its flame has an affinity to their own, and their potential expression of divinity. Here, the visitors are charged with renewed hope and spiritual vitality; they are made consciously aware of the truth of "life everlasting" and the miraculous potentials that the Resurrection Flame can generate within those who invoke it. The purpose of this focus is to continue to pour into all levels of human consciousness, emotional, mental, physical and etheric, and all the evolutions that belong to this planet, the reality of the powers of the Resurrection Flame.

Mankind, for the most part, has accepted the resurrection of Jesus as a "miracle" only possible for him and have not availed themselves of the use of that miraculous flame to restore their own bodies to perfection. Rather, they have submitted to disease, disintegration, decay and finally so-called "death" as natural processes of Life. However, to keep alive the feeling of the power of the resurrection in the consciousness of unascended mankind, beloved Jesus/Sananda, Nada and Mother Mary continuously send forth into the atmosphere of Earth that victorious radiation from this temple.

The Flame of Resurrection is the hope of redemption for the entire human race, quickening the vibratory action of the light within the cells of the body, and enabling the inner light to throw off the appearance of limitation. The substance of the Resurrection Flame flows through the inner bodies of those who invite it, as well as through the physical body.

The Sixth Ray

Message of Love from Lord Sananda Together with Lady Nada

Greetings, my beloveds, I am Lord Sananda, and I come accompanied by my beloved Nada. It is indeed a great joy and honor for us to be given this opportunity to greet all of you who are reading this life-changing material and connect with you in a very personal way. We desire to speak to your hearts and souls of our favorite subjects, the topics of Self Love and the powers of the Resurrection Flame, whose guardianship we have been entrusted with as our service to Life.

Some of you read many books, with the hope of finding the magical keys that will create within your soul the openings to assist your return back home to the dimensions of Love and Light that you once knew. So many of you are yearning to meet and work with us again face-to-face and live the "real life" beyond the human shackles of the illusion of separation.

Know, my beloveds, all that you ever wanted and dreamed of is waiting your allowance and recognition to be born and to be bestowed upon you. All the wondrous gifts, the limitlessness and the divine faculties that are of the "I AM Presence," are simply bursting with the desire to be activated and restored within you. In truth, there is nothing outside yourself you can acquire that can permanently satisfy your deepest longings, at least not for long.

But, dear ones, you have to ask and allow yourself to receive. Allow some time every day to contemplate and focus on the object of your desires. You all know this, but very few of you take time to apply what you learn in the books you read. You are Creators, and you have to create what you want with the love of your heart, your intention and focus. It simply does not happen on its own, without your focus, without your asking, without setting your intention and without activating the feeling of gratitude for the receivership of the fruit of your creation.

Now with the limited space allotted us in this book, we will do our best to give you the maximum. And Oh! There is so much more we would like to share with you. Thus, we encourage you to come to our retreat at night, the Temple of Resurrection near Jerusalem, to commune with us personally, to feel our hearts and to get what is not in the book directly from us. It is our service and great pleasure to teach you your next step, and the next one, to assist you in attaining your mastery. This is an invitation, beloveds.

It is so important that you begin focusing on knowing and loving yourself. How can you expect to create Divine Union with your "I AM" through Ascension if you are not dedicated to truly knowing that part of yourself you want to merge with? Beginning to know the Self is to Love it; it cannot be otherwise. This is exactly what will free you from all your burdens, sorrows and limitations. "Knowing and loving your innermost being will bring you everything you ever longed for and desired." Therefore, the statement "Know Thyself" is the most wondrous and profound statement that exists in your language.

We wish to give you some explanations about the inner workings of the "I AM Presence" so that you can gain a greater understanding in accessing it.

On the third dimension, you have had many adventures and experiences in separation. You have collected doubts, fears, confusion, misunderstandings and you do not always know what choices to make or when to make them. You do not always know your purpose, your destiny or your next step. There is always a place in your consciousness where you entertain self-doubt and non-knowingness about many things in your life. You often find yourself in a physical body on an outrageous plane of existence without a plan, without direction or instruction.

For most of you, you do not even have a plan "A", never mind a plan "B". **Being in the now is certainly a good plan, especially if you do not have full awareness.** You have been noticing lately that you are more and more in the now moment with whatever you are doing. When you live in the now moment, you enter into the consciousness of the God "I AM" within you. It is that part of you which holds the agenda of your divine plan for all eternity and also for this lifetime. When you make plans from the mind or the ego, you find they do not always work out and you are not always able to follow through.

We are going to reveal some of what has been mysterious within you, that you may embrace the great mystery that you are. First, we will tell you that the "I AM Presence" is a resonance and a vibration "inside of you," from within the heart and soul. You will feel it very powerfully in the vicinity of the heart and throat area. You will also feel it revolving all of the chakras at the same time when it is activated and open.

What activates the "I AM Presence" is the choices you make. When you use your power and your desires to make a choice clear and simple, the "I AM" is involved. When there are no doubts, fears or hesitation about that choice, no issues arise to obstruct the choice being brought forth and you have a completely clear energy. When you choose in total clarity, and there is no separation present, the "I AM" is activated and completely free to express.

The truth is that there are only a few issues you have to work out in order to realize your mastery. Isn't this interesting? What if we tell you that you can count those issues on one hand! Most of you already know and believe you are going to bring forth mastery and Ascension in this lifetime. You do not know yet how, you do not know yet all the steps and you will not be informed because the steps to mastery are miracles that are revealed in precise moments and are meant to accelerate your progress. These will always be moments of wondrous surprises and expansion. They are meant to be "secrets" until the moment of that revelation. Who you are is not only God portraying "beingness," but you as a Creator.

> **The beingness and the creatorship go hand in hand.**
> **Be bold and start bringing forth all of your dreams;**
> **it is time to make them come true!**

Now let us talk about the power of Resurrection, which means to bring back or restore to a normal condition. This understanding brings the knowledge out of the miraculous into a working law, with which those using it can be restored to wholeness. Witnessing the action of the Resurrection Flame through the bodies of those who have been resurrected from the dead or those with extreme physical conditions, we see death give way to life, the normal condition for every soul.

If a dormant bulb lying in the ground through the long winter beneath snow and ice can be stirred to life by the Resurrection Flame each spring, and direct its shoots and flowers through the soil giving forth beauty and fragrance, it should be a great hope and example to all of you. If a simple bulb can externalize its immaculate concept through the Resurrection Flame, so can you externalize your mastery. In fact, you can do this in a much greater way, if only you would spend time invoking it daily in your life, for your projects, for your gardens and for everything you want to create and resurrect.

The principle is the same for the bulb as it is for each of you in your life. Each year around Easter, the Flame of Resurrection is amplified in greater measure for over 40 days to create the miracles of spring for nature, for humans and for all life on the planet. The Resurrection Flame is also available the rest of the year to everyone to use and invoke. ***It is limitless and free for the asking!*** What better deal could you find on the Internet? Did you ever contemplate what makes all of nature suddenly wake-up for a new round of beingness in the spring? Of course, it is this wondrous golden flame!

Take now a moment to allow yourself to feel the Resurrection Flame burst within you. Invoke it fully until you can feel it. The simple affirmation, "I AM the Resurrection and the Life" was given to me by one of my mentors, the Great Divine Director, in my last incarnation prior to starting my public life in the land of Galilee. This was such a key for me and I was so grateful for the gift of this affirmation. With this simple sentence, I built a momentum of the Flame of Resurrection in my inner bodies to such an extent, that this very momentum allowed me to resurrect my body after the crucifixion.

Say it now aloud or silently in your heart three times. Now feel the current of hope alive within you, for within your heart you know that there is the seed of a divine plan and destiny waiting to burst forth and externalize itself, to make each of you, step-by-step, a Christed being. This seed in you is, by far, so much more powerful than the tiny kernel held within the pattern of the crocus or the early violet.

I am Sananda, together with Nada, we bless you and send you our Eternal Flame of Cosmic Love. Accept from us the gift of the Resurrection Flame and use it to discover its wonderful miraculous producing powers!

The Seven Sacred Flames

Solar Plexus Chakra

The Sixth Ray

Prayer for Sixth Ray Healing

Invocation to the Flame of Resurrection

I AM the Resurrection and the Life
of my eternal Freedom in the Light.

I AM the Resurrection and the Life
of my physical body's perfect blueprint

I AM the Resurrection and the Life
of my emotional body's perfect blueprint

I AM the Resurrection and the Life
of my mental body's perfect blueprint

I AM the Resurrection and the Life
of my etheric body's perfect blueprint

I AM the Resurrection and the Life
of my spiritual body's perfect blueprint

I AM the Resurrection and the Life
of the Ascended Masters Purity and Love.

I AM the Resurrection and the Life
of the healing powers of the Sacred Flames.

I AM the Resurrection and the Life
of my Immortal Perfection and
Illumined Love of the Cosmic Christ.

I AM the Resurrection and the Life
of the powers of the Sacred Fire within me,
restoring all the wondrous gifts of my Divine Essence.

Discourse from Adama
with Jesus/Sananda and Lady Nada

Group - What is Adama planning for us tonight?

Aurelia - I had a talk with Adama this afternoon, as I did not have any idea what we were going to talk about this evening. Adama would like to talk about the Resurrection Flame and its healing attributes. This wondrous Flame is not well known to the majority of the people in this dimension, even to those who have heard about it. They often do not know how to use it. The Resurrection Flame is one of the seven major Flames of God that have been available to people on this planet since the beginning of time. It has an action of its own, but also carries another aspect of healing.

The whole world is in desperate need of many kinds and levels of healing at this time. The word healing has a broad meaning, including many aspects and many levels. Before we can be whole and express the fullness of the Light of the "I AM" again, we have to heal all aspects of ourselves on deeper levels until completion. People hear about healing in so many different ways on the third dimension, but true healing is little understood. In fact, in order to understand true healing, it would be wise to learn about the attributes of the seven major Flames of God constantly flooding this planet to nurture and sustain Life.

The understanding that Adama would like to convey this evening is about healing on a higher level, true healing, not just a temporary solution which you have to resolve permanently at a later time. The Flame of Resurrection is another extraordinary tool among others, which is free, easy to use and very effective. Unfortunately, it is not used by the majority of the people because the knowledge is forgotten.

The emerald green vibration of the Fifth Ray of Healing and the energies of the Great Jade Temple is one tool, but there are many other awesome ones. The more aware we become of these tools and the more we use them, the more we can transform our lives with ease and grace. Adama wants to give us a greater understanding of The Resurrection Flame, discussing electrons and how we can raise our consciousness by using those tools.

There are seven days of the week, seven notes on the musical scale, seven main chakras, seven main endocrine glands and seven main organs and systems in the body, etc. The list is quite long. Do you get the picture? Each one of these Rays represents a specific color vibration and is connected with one of the names I just mentioned. For example, each day of the week is amplified with the energies of one of the Rays with its corresponding color vibration. Each note in a musical octave represents a specific color and Ray energy. Each one of the seven glands and the seven main organs in your body is connected with one of the seven main chakras, which in turn is connected to one of the Seven Flames. The Flame of Resurrection is something you can use through eternity and always benefit from it. I now bring Adama.

𝒜𝑑𝑎𝑚𝑎 - Greetings my dearest friends, this is your friend and mentor Adama. It is a pleasure for me and my team to be with you once again today to present pearls of wisdom and knowledge to those who want to expand their awareness and understanding of God's wondrous attributes. I am here with the guardians of the Flame of Resurrection, Lord Jesus/Sananda with his beloved Nada, known in your world as Mary Magdalene in her last incarnation. They have come to beam the radiance of their Love to all of you, and share with you the truth which has been kept from you for so long.

What you have been taught, the real truth about God and your divinity in your short incarnation on this planet so far, is limited compared to what there is to know. There is much knowledge at your disposal today to be embraced and understood for the unfoldment of your consciousness.

Most of you have experienced thousands of incarnations on this planet, and in your current incarnation, you have been presented with only a few pearls of true knowledge. This is now changing. Tonight we will share another one of these spiritual treasures to assist your healing.

The Flame of Resurrection is not uniquely a Healing Flame; its sphere of action is vast, and in our short time together, we can only cover a general understanding. It was the Flame of Resurrection that the Master Jesus used to resurrect his own body in the tomb after the crucifixion 2,000 years ago. This alone should give you a clue. When you contemplate its greater meaning, what does resurrection really mean? What it did for this great Avatar, can also work for you. The attributes of this Flame have not diminished; on the contrary, it has gathered more momentum since that time.

Although this Flame is always active, Easter time is when its energy doubles in intensity for the benefit of mankind. The Flame of Resurrection, as a Sixth Ray activity, also embodies the energies of Selfless Service and Ministration. That is what Jesus embodied and demonstrated by his life and his selfless service to humanity. He remained in this holy calling for the whole dispensation of the Aquarian Age.

His experience with the Flame of Resurrection was not unique; he simply knew how to use its life-giving energies. Now that you have evolved your consciousness to a greater level of understanding, it is important for you to start using this flame for your own transformation. There are many tools at your disposal to ease your life and to accelerate your evolutionary path. You

The Sixth Ray

simply need to be aware of them and diligently start using them every day.

When you desire healing in your body, use the energy of the Resurrection Flame to accomplish this by taking into your body a much higher frequency than you already carry. A superficial, temporary healing is not what you really want. You need something that is uplifting and permanent. You want your healing to reflect your divine perfection.

When the master Jesus said, "I AM the Resurrection and the Life," he was not talking about his human self in incarnation. He was teaching the divine law of the mighty "I AM" that lives in your Sacred Heart, not yet fully expressed in your present state of awareness. Understand that the Resurrection Flame is an energy you can easily use for your benefit by focusing on it, by invoking it and by playing with it. Be creative!

Group - *It sounds awesome to me. Until Aurelia mentioned it, I had never heard of it. How can we make it work in our lives?*

Adama - It is one of the many attributes of God. You can resurrect your finances, you can resurrect your bodies, you can resurrect family harmony and you can resurrect a great number of things you want to expand in your life.

You can use the words "I AM," knowing that it is the unlimited aspect of you, or you can say something like, "From the Lord God of my being, I call forth now to receive a great infusion of Resurrection Flame in every cell, atom, and electron in my physical body, my emotional body, my mental body, my etheric body, my body elemental and all my subtle bodies. I wish to heal and resurrect all aspects of my life. *(Name other things you personally want to resurrect such as finances, talents, memories, harmony, etc.)*" The sky is not even the limit on how you can use this energy. If you experience lack of any kind in your life, if your body is not in a state of luminosity and immortality, if you are not yet manifesting absolute divine beauty, youth and perfection, it means that the electrons composing your physical structure are still suffering levels of distortions. Call the Resurrection Flame to come to your rescue.

Group - *How often do we need to do this?*

Adama - In your dimension, where energy moves so slowly unlike in ours where creation is instant, you need to focus on what you want to create several times a day, until you obtain the desired results. You also need to add feelings of love and gratitude to the focus of your creation. If you focus only once, your chance of manifesting what you want is rather slim. It is not a question of repeating affirmations like a parrot, but sending your loving thoughts throughout the day as you go about your business, with the absolute knowingness that your creation is manifesting through your love and intention. This is how the laws of manifestation work.

If you choose to do affirmations, which are very helpful, be sure that you repeat them, not as a supplication, but as a statement of loving intention, with the full intensity of emotion from your heart, infusing the object of your desire with as much faith and gratitude as possible. It is always helpful to visualize the Resurrection Flame as a golden orange-yellow energy, luminescent in color like a summer sunset. Make it real. Give it life in your heart and mind, because as you visualize it, so it becomes. If you want healing, infuse the problem you want to heal with that energy, and be sure to sustain it long enough to obtain the results you desire.

The energies of the Flames are also connected to each one of your chakras. As you evolve your consciousness, you will discover many more chakras will be activated, and you will become acquainted with many more than just seven flames. All the flames work individually and together in a synchronistic way, like rainbows of light to assist and sustain you. Think of energies such as the Flame of Joy, the Flame of Harmony, the Flame of Comfort and Peace, etc. Their wonders are simply endless.

Next, I would like to share some understanding of electrons.

The smallest manifestation of life can be measured in terms which men would understand as electrons. These electrons represent particles of energy from the body of Prime Creator, which is eternally self-sustained, indestructible, self-luminous and intelligent. Electrons are pure universal light substance, responding like lightning to the creative powers of both God and men. In varying forms, they make up the atoms of the physical world. Interstellar space is filled with this pure "light-essence." The number of electrons, which combine with each other in a specific atom, is the result of, and determined by conscious "thought."

The rate at which they whirl around the central core is the result of and determined by "feelings." The intensity of the whirling motion within the central core is the "breath of God." Therefore, the most concentrated activity of "Divine Love," the energy that grows your food, the substance you find in the third dimension, is all created by various manifestations of electrons that have been qualified differently. Everything is made of the same "stuff," called electrons. All electrons come from prime Source energy as "Love."

Electrons are created as energy particles from etheric planes of consciousness; their energy is neutral and totally at the service of Life. They manifest in form only when they become qualified by other conscious parts of life. Electrons take various forms, shapes and densities according to how they are qualified. In your world, when you qualify energy with less than pure Love, when you create with fear, anger or greed, you are misusing electrons and creating distortions in their original purpose to serve Life. This miscreation then become yours to own as karma. You have to live with the programming you have qualified the electrons with. When you balance all your debts to life with Love, you purify all the electrons you have misused. This is what you call the "working out of karma."

Take note, my dear brothers and sisters, of what I am going to say next. This is most important for you to remember always.

God gives you on a daily basis an unlimited number of electrons with which to create your life, and you are always free to create in any way you wish. According to what you create with your thoughts, intentions and emotions, your life reflects how you use the electrons available to you. In general, humanity does not understand the right use of electrons, in other words, the right use of energy at their disposal. This knowledge is forgotten. By misusing energy as you do on the surface of the Earth, you create much pain and difficulty for yourself, for your planet and for everyone evolving here.

Group - Do we misqualify the use of that energy through self-doubt, judgment, fear, negative emotions, and actions that are not expressing love?

Adama - Yes, electrons want to respond to Love. When you misqualify them with vibrations other than Love or Joy, they become distorted, and that distortion becomes your cosmic responsibility. How do you think the electrons used for nuclear energy or other types of destruction feel? Remember, they carry prime Creator consciousness and intelligence. Because they are commissioned to serve Life unconditionally, they have to serve mankind in whatever way mankind chooses to use them. These electrons, more often than not, remain embedded in the negativity of mankind, sometimes for eons. This is not what they want or what they were created for; they have to painfully submit to that misuse.

Mankind can use electrons to create an absolute paradise for themselves, for the planet, for everything around them, or they can use them to destroy themselves and their world. This is the experiment of free will on this planet. Not all planets have free will to the extent you have here on Earth. The misuse of free will has been a very painful experience for humanity. This is why the right use of electrons is so important to understand. The Resurrection Flame can help you purify the electrons you have misused back into harmony. Like everything else, all Flames of God are also made of electrons.

Group - *What you are saying is that if we are oriented in fear or negative emotion, the energy we conduct is being misused. From Creator Source, electrons are imbued with Love and alive with consciousness, flowing to us for our use.*

Adama - Exactly, it is constant everywhere in all Universes. Electrons represent the energy you use to create your life daily. If you misuse electrons or energy, it creates fields of darkness around and inside of you. If you misuse these to create fear within yourself or project this kind of energy to others, in doubts and judgments, the electrons of your own body become distorted and eventually create diseases, illnesses, lack of vitality and aging, etc.

Group - *How does using the Resurrection Flame correspond to our needs, as we are moving into mastery, gaining the wisdom and understanding from our experiences?*

Adama - First of all, you need to understand that the Resurrection Flame is not the only Flame nurturing Life. You cannot freely misuse God's energy without consequences. When you qualify God's energy with Love, the electrons start flowing in a different manner, creating harmony, because that is their nature. Your nature is divine and so is theirs.

You have to work with your emotions and become very aware of your thought patterns and your actions. You can invoke the Flame of Resurrection to assist you in restoring harmony in your life and healing all your issues. When you begin to re-qualify energy or electrons with the Flames of God, the electrons will begin to spin clockwise instead of counter-clockwise. This inner work needs to be embraced as a way of life, "progress in action," not something you do only once in a while. This is your most important assignment and the key to the spiritual freedom you long for.

The gifts of this Flame are impersonal, not limited to one being 2,000 years ago, but to all the children of the Creator at any time, anywhere. Some people use it for their finances: "I am the resurrection and the life of my finances." Others use it for their healing: "I am the resurrection and the life of my perfect health." When you start using it, many things will be shown to your awareness for your spiritual growth. Before you can receive what you want, you may need to weed the garden of your consciousness. As you focus on the object of your desires, what needs to be re-aligned will be shown to you, and as you change your consciousness, your life will change for the better.

You know, old age and degeneration have never been natural attributes of life. The appearance of your physical body is determined by the amount of light carried within your lower vehicles, the emotional, mental, etheric and physical bodies. The natural emanation of light through these body systems forms the protecting wall referred to as the tube of light around you. When the electrons move slowly in their particular organs and cells, they draw less light from your Higher Self, creating resistance and a weaker light stream. How much vitality you are going to have in your body and how you are going to start feeling has to do with how fast the electrons can spin in your body.

The more toxins you have and the less light you hold, the slower the electrons spin, encouraging old age, disease, misalignment and malfunction of your organs, glands and systems. In time, your whole body begins to experience aging. In Telos, we have attained immortality because we learned to keep ourselves and everything we do in our physical lives, in our mental attitudes and our emotional bodies totally clear of negativity. We clear ourselves regularly with the many tools we are teaching you. Our electrons are spinning at the speed that keeps our bodies always young and beautiful. Immortality is not such a mystery once you begin to understand it, but an unfoldment of "real Life" that is divine and natural.

Group - *Do masters ever make mistakes?*

Adama - You have to realize that when you talk about masters and mastery, there are various levels. There are masters of fourth dimension, there are masters of fifth dimension and there are masters of all dimensions. In each dimension, one is learning greater and greater levels of mastery. For example, if you talk about masters in the fourth dimension, yes, they can make mistakes, but it is also their learning process, as for you. You are learning mostly by your mistakes. The mistakes they make are not very serious, because they have greater wisdom and they work under the guidance of masters of higher dimensions. At the higher levels, we do things in groups and unity, so that we always get the benefit of the wisdom of the whole and from those who have a greater spiritual attainment.

Whatever happens in your life, let's say you lost your house in a fire, or were in an accident and lost a leg, or have become blind, or lost large sums of money, or suffered a broken relationship, no matter what it is, whether the challenge is small or big, instead of being angry, depressed and bitter, what if you were to say, "What is it that I can I learn and heal from this experience?"

Surrendering to the lessons you are supposed to learn from challenges is the key to walking through them quickly. Your life changes and you do not have to grapple with the same lessons. You can move on to those that bring you much more joy. Lessons do not always have to be difficult to learn; they become difficult for those who chose to totally ignore them.

> **There are those who have had lifetime after lifetime of not wanting to see, to know or to have anything to do with their lessons.**

Then comes a time when life will no longer allow you to ignore the promptings of your soul, and this is when life can become difficult. It is not required that you grapple with lessons forever. You can move through them quickly until you start outpicturing the manifestation of the beautiful diamond light that you are, and then attain your enlightenment. The lessons you are learning manifest because "you" have created them in the first place. It is not that God sends you lessons to annoy you. It is through the misuse of your free will that you have created your lessons and your reality.

As you take responsibility and look at your lessons and say, "What is it that I need to learn out of this mess I have created, and what blessings are in it? What is the gift?" Any negative or difficult situation you experience in life can be turned back into something wonderful, if it is approached the right way. Even a disease or a financial loss can open the opportunity for greater blessings to manifest once you open your consciousness to receive them. How many people gain great wisdom from their illnesses or a relationship that has ended?

For example, there are still a great number of people mistreating animals in your society because, in their consciousness, they are far removed from the truth of the Oneness of all life. Many still live in the illusion that animals are lower forms of life, right? The abuse of animals allowed to take place in your society, inflicting on their souls experiences of ruthless slaughter, abandonment, caging, chaining, lab experimentations, etc., does not reflect the qualities of enlightenment.

When people mistreat or hurt animals, they deny that they are made of the same electrons from the prime Creator. Once you fully realize that everything that exists lives out of God's energy, and primal energy is all the same, you become fully aware that you can "never" hurt any part of life without hurting yourself equally and bearing the karma.

Group - *Let me also add, Adama, it is not just the animal kingdom, but the plant and mineral kingdoms, the nature spirits and the elementals that suffer at the hands of unenlightened people.*

Adama - Oh, of course. I only use the animals as one example. Do those polluting and raping the planet think they are not accountable for their actions and free of consequences? For the ones raping, polluting your planet, polluting your waterways, polluting the air, your very breath of Life are going to suffer the return of their creation. As you sow, so shall you reap! Some people on Earth are still doing much harm to the planet and to their human brothers and sisters. In time, they will reap the consequences of their actions. No one can ever escape the great law of divine justice.

Group - Another misunderstanding floating around is that everyone is going to make it into the fifth dimension as the Earth shifts into the Ascension state in 2012.

Adama - Everyone who has shifted their consciousness to unconditional love and has diligently fulfilled all other requirements for Ascension will certainly make it along with the planet. But others will have to experience their creation and continue their evolution until they "get it," and shift to Love and unity consciousness. Much assistance and mercy will be granted to those choosing the Ascension at this time, but those not choosing this fervently are not going to make it in this cycle. Basically, most people on the planet are good and loving people, even if they are not yet awakened spiritually.

Those who create again and again so many problems for others and for the planet will not qualify for ascension and they are going to experience the return of their miscreation. For them, the Ascension becomes a possibility in another cycle. Everyone will have an opportunity to make it to the fifth dimension who chooses to, but not everyone is making that choice.

I invite everyone to make this choice in your heart. Do you want to come now or do you want to wait for another long cycle?

Because the corridors of Ascension are opening wide at this time, it does not mean they will remain open forever. The corridors of Ascension were closed for a long time for surface dwellers, and no one knows when they will close or open again. This decision is not within our jurisdiction. It could take another several thousand years before there is another such opportunity for Ascension. We urge you to not remain on the picket fence in a state of indecision. Make your choice now and be committed to your choice.

The Sixth Ray

Let me clarify something. There are those on Earth right now, because of their age, such as your senior citizens, who have made the choice to come into the Ascension on the inner plane, but they do not qualify for this in this lifetime. There is too much for them yet to clear and understand; some dear souls have old and sick bodies and did not have the opportunity to fully open their understanding.

At a soul level, they are gentle people who have been harmless. Many of them will leave their body, but this does not mean they are not coming into the Ascension. The divine grace for them is that they will be given another opportunity for incarnation in the "new world" we are moving into, and the process of ascension in the next life will be much easier and joyful for them. This is the divine grace accorded to them.

As people on this planet move into the fourth and fifth dimensional consciousness, they will continue to have children. Most civilizations in the higher dimensions can have children. Many of these souls will ascend physically in their next life experience. The right opportunity will be at hand for every soul.

Now I would like to expand more on the use the Resurrection Flame to rejuvenate the physical body and the subject of immortality. It is important to understand the use of the Resurrection Flame and all the other flames. The Resurrection energy is a key vibration for attaining immortality of the physical body. If you want to make the shift with your body, without going through the process of physical death, the Resurrection Flame will greatly assist you. You see, when you take a real interest in your own evolution and allow the Resurrection Flame to pass through your body regularly, you begin to embody a greater level of harmony, beauty and vitality. Immortality starts by expressing more youthfulness and vitality within your lifestream.

The soul who has attained a certain level of maturity should be more beautiful and exquisite in face and form as the years pass. The aging process you experience as you get older is naturally going to change in the years to come. It is already changing for many. As you get older and integrate more light into your consciousness, you will begin to express more beauty and perfection in your physical body. Does this make your heart sing?

Creating distortions in the body, losing vitality and looking older is not a divine attribute. We encourage you to start contemplating the Flame of Resurrection with its ability to reverse aging and to make you glow. Can you imagine if every cell, atom and electron in your body were to start glowing with the Flame of Resurrection, you would become luminous and radiant? Your body would take on the exquisite beauty and all attributes of your divine Self.

As you age, you will become increasingly more beautiful and divine in your physical form. This is what we have attained in Telos, and this is my main message for you tonight. Since we are basically all the same genetically, what we have attained, you can all attain as well. Some of us in Telos have lived for thousands of years without any sign of aging. The Resurrection Flame is a major factor in maintaining our youthfulness. Are you ready for the meditation?

The Sixth Ray

Meditation

Journey to the Temple of Resurrection in the Fifth Dimension

Adama with Lord Sananda and Lady Nada

We now invite all of you to take a journey in consciousness to the Temple of Resurrection near Jerusalem. One of the functions of this temple is to assist humanity with the energies of true resurrection, which takes place at many levels. In your immediate and future evolution, you are no longer looking to simply manifest superficial or temporary healings for various problems that burden you, whether they are of physical, emotional, mental or spiritual nature. What you need to do is infuse the energy of Resurrection in your body and consciousness, knowing that it will assist in raising your vibration above the frequency of your present life circumstances. The Flame of Resurrection is available to you at any time and it is free. All it takes is a bit of your time, your focus and your love to invoke it forth and work with it.

Now connect in your heart to your "I AM Presence" as you take several deep breaths. Ask your light body to descend over you and take you in consciousness to the Resurrection Temple; it knows how to get you there. If you desire to come along with us on this journey, I invite you to formulate your intent in your heart now. *(Pause)*

This temple is created of substance which resembles "mother of pearl." It is circular in design, glowing as a sun from a distance, looking like vapors of pearls and golden sunlight all around it. In various places, it reflects the luminosity of other Flames. Ask your guides to take you there in your light body and become aware of this place in your consciousness. Now see yourself there, entering a large room called "The Hall of Resurrection." It contains many chambers and doorways. A large number of beings from different dimensions use this hall . It vibrates at various high frequencies in different places to accommodate those of other dimensions. Now see a group of beings, guardians of the temple, approaching to welcome you and accompany you for your experience here.

People of the third dimension are taken into chambers designed for their level of vibrational tolerance. This temple is well attended; many souls from this galaxy and beyond who visit this planet, come here to recharge. Breathe in this wonderful Golden Flame energy and let it infuse every particle of your being. *(Pause)*

This Flame will assist the expansion of your consciousness, your understanding of life and evolution to a greater level than the one you presently hold. Breathe in and integrate the consciousness and the energy of the Resurrection. Breathe it into every cell, every atom and electron of all your bodies. Use the Resurrection Flame on a regular basis and it will continue to expand within you unto eternity. Beings of higher dimensions are still using it to expand their consciousness at higher levels.

Stay with us for a while in the Hall of Resurrection and with those of the temple who have graciously volunteered to accompany you. Millions of Resurrection Flame angels nurture and minister to humanity each day, especially those who ask and make conscious contact with them and with this Flame. You have access not only to the Flame, but also to all the wonderful angels willing to work with you on a one-to-one basis, to nurture and to love you back to your spiritual freedom.

As you stand in the wonderment of this golden hall, you see countless golden Flames of Resurrection in all shapes and sizes burning bright perpetually to assist the Earth and evolving humanity.

Walk around the hall to gaze at all the wonders you see. As you walk, your guide directs you to a specific circle reserved for Earth's surface dwellers. The circle is made of Flames of various sizes and shapes that look like different varieties of flowers. One of these Resurrection seats is calling you to sit quietly and soak in the energies into your bodies. Now choose the seat that is calling you. It may feel like you are sitting in a lotus flower, but it is the Resurrection Flame taking the shape and appearance of a flower. This golden flame enfolds you completely to raise your energies and bring healing and comfort to your soul. As you sit and contemplate the wonders of your experience, keep breathing in and absorbing all the energies you can. Feel it permeating every aspect of your being.

Now take a few minutes to make a conscious request of what you would like to clear and what areas of your life you would like to resurrect the most. Focus on the unique gift you are receiving today, being nurtured and loved by the guides and angels that accompany you. Breathe in more, because you want to take as much of this energy back with you into your physical body.

Feel your body being imprinted with the Resurrection energy and become aware of how it affects you. Awaken your sensory bodies to feel it more deeply. Feel the joy that it brings to your heart. Absorb all you can and feel how much lighter you are becoming in that seat. It feels as though the angels are carrying you on wings of light. Consciously set your intention for this wonderful flame to literally lift you up and out of the predicaments you are trying to heal and balance.

Don't hesitate to invite the Master Jesus/Sananda with his beloved Nada and their momentum of the Resurrection Flame to assist you; they are masters and guardians of this Flame. If Sananda as Jesus could raise his own body from the dead and use the same energy to raise Lazarus from the dead, he can certainly assist you in great measure. What he did, you can do also, but you have to build your own momentum over a period of time. You can use this Flame to literally resurrect your own body to an absolute divine state of perfection, beauty, radiance, luminosity, immortality and limitlessness.

When you feel complete, return to full consciousness. Get up from your seat and return to meet with us again at the entrance of the Hall of Resurrection. We are taking you back to your physical body, but the connection to the Flame will remain. You are most welcome to return and take a seat in the Resurrection Temple any time you wish and receive all the benefits each time. You may go every day or as often as you please.

The Elixirs of Immortality come from the Resurrection Flame.

We now send you love, peace, harmony and healing from Telos and from the members of our community of Light. Know that we are with you at all times and we are as close to you as your call. Any time you want to connect with us, our hearts are open. We are your brothers and sisters, and we love you very much. And so be it.

Aurelia - Thank you so much, Adama, for that wonderful, wonderful message and meditation and for introducing us to the Resurrection Flame and its many attributes for our lives. What a wonderful gift and what a blessing! We also express our heartfelt gratitude, Nada and Sananda, for your presence and the contribution of your love and radiance here today. We love you so much, Adama, Sananda and Nada. Thank you so much for being the wonderful teachers that you are.

The Sixth Ray

Adama - It has been our delight and great pleasure. We have been looking forward to the day we could introduce this teaching to surface people. We love you all so very much also. You know, whatever one does or neglects to do never goes unnoticed in our realm. You are creating by your work and your diligence wonderful pearls of Love. Be assured that someday, you will be reaping the harvest of these pearls. Whatever you create in Love you will reap in Love!

We are very grateful in Telos for this opportunity to be heard and read, and to have a voice on the surface, at last. We have waited for this type of opportunity for centuries. We long to reconnect "heart-to-heart" with our family on the surface. The bridge between our civilization and your civilization has been created, but it is much stronger on our side. You have yet to strengthen your bridges with us. Heart connections must be made with a much larger number of people before we can emerge among you tangibly. When enough people are ready and willing to accept our teachings, we will make our presence known visibly and publicly.

Group - *Thank you so much, we are most grateful for your love and your teachings. We can't wait to hear more at another time. Again thank you, beloved friends, it has been worth every moment. Until we meet again, blessings to you, Adama, Sananda, Nada, and all other members of our Telosian family.*

Master Saint Germain

Chapter Seven

The Seventh Ray:

The Violet Flame of Transmutation

Main God qualities and actions of the Violet Flame:
Freedom, Transmutation, Transformation, Diplomacy, Ceremony and Application of the science of true alchemy.

Corresponding Chakra: Seat of the Soul
Color: Violet
Corresponding Stone: Amethyst, Violet Fluorite

Chohan of the Seventh Ray:
Master Saint Germain, also known as the God of Freedom
His Retreats: Transylvania, Romania, and the Great Violet Flame Temple, Jackson Peak in, Wyoming, USA.

Archangels of the Seventh Ray with Divine Complement:
Zadkiel and Amethyst
Their Retreat: Over the Island of Cuba

Elohim of the Seventh Ray with Divine Complement:
Arcturus and Victoria
Their Retreat: Near Luanda, Angola, Africa

Note: Let us mention Omri Tas, the ruler of the Violet planet, where the Seventh Ray Violet Flame is generated for this universe. Let us acknowledge his Presence and his perpetual service to this Sacred Flame. He is also available to assist us in the correct use of the Violet Flame of Transmutation when we include his presence in our invocations.

The Home of Master Saint Germain

Nestled deep in the beautiful natural forests and foothills of the Carpathian Mountains near the Hungarian/Romanian border, we come upon the Baronial Manor house in the heart of Transylvania, the home of one of humanity's greatest benefactors, the Master Saint Germain. His service to life began long before the crying need of the people of Earth for freedom was aroused. Many of his incarnations took place in the immediate neighborhood of this estate. Through the centuries, many benefactors of the human race have been entertained in his gracious home, though they were not always fully aware of the status of their host. Among its many interesting features, the lovely old home holds priceless treasures that mark the milestones and progress of mankind's journey.

Embodiments of Master Saint Germain

- In the 11th century BC, Saint Germain was embodied as the prophet Samuel.

- Saint Germain was embodied as Saint Joseph, the father of Jesus and the husband of Mary.

- In the late 3rd century, he was embodied as Saint Alban, the first martyr of Britain. Alban lived in England during the persecutions of Christians under the Roman emperor Diocletian.

- In the 5th century, Saint Germain was embodied as Merlin, the great alchemist, prophet and counselor at the court of King Arthur.

- As Roger Bacon (1220-1292), the beloved Saint Germain was philosopher, Franciscan monk, teacher and scientist.

- As Christopher Columbus (1451-1506), he discovered America.

- As Francis Bacon (1561-1626), he was philosopher, statesman, and literary master. Research demonstrates that he was the author of the Shakespeare's plays and the son of Queen Elizabeth and Lord Leicester.

- Desiring above all else to liberate God's people, Saint Germain was granted a dispensation from the Lords of Karma to return to Earth in a physical body. He appeared as "le Comte de Saint Germain," a "miraculous person" who dazzled the courts of 18th and 19th century in Europe, where he was known as the "Wonder man of Europe."

For more detailed information about the Masters and their Retreats, consult the book by Mark and Elizabeth Clare Prophet, compiled and edited by Annice Booth, Summit University Press.

Excerpts from Lord Zadkiel

Those of you who know about the use of the Violet Flame have a special opportunity now to draw forth from your Causal Body all the knowledge you have accumulated from the past. This flame acts as does the sunshine, "impersonally" and instantly whenever and wherever it is called forth. Let that Violet Fire blaze up in, through and around your four body systems, and especially through your brain structure, commanding it to transmute the hard and unforgiving thoughts and feelings in your etheric, mental and emotional bodies. These "hard core" feelings create most of your distress.

Let them be replaced by grateful, joyous receptive feelings which open your world to the goodness of God, and make you a mighty magnet drawing to you all the good God wants you to have, all the good you once knew. Let the feelings of gratitude to the Holy Father for these gifts so flood your world that you will be able to outpicture more quickly the Divine Perfection you wish to attain. When you want the Violet Fire of freedom's love, mercy and compassion to act in your world, start invoking it in the name and authority of your own I AM Presence. This Flame becomes more powerful each time it is called forth.

Long ago, on Atlantis and Lemuria, we externalized a gigantic focus of this Violet Fire on each continent. Its radiating flame was seen by the physical sight for a distance of a thousand miles in all directions. It is our earnest intention to recreate these wonders in the era of the Seventh Golden Age.

Lovely ones, the Violet Flame is absolutely real. This flame is your freedom as it blazes in, through and around you. Invoke it daily and let go of emotional, mental, etheric and physical chaos. Accept the divine justice which is the heritage of your being, to become a God and Goddess on this Earth, and then achieve the full glory of Ascended Master status.

Do not limit the Powers of your I AM Presence.

Master Saint Germain

Please, beloved ones, become re-acquainted with that the glorious Presence of which you are an essence, "The Magic Presence." Its wonderful omnipotent powers are willing and ready to act through you at all times. As your human self, you could not possibly attempt to rehabilitate the human race. Of course not! But your Presence can! Your infinite, individualized "I AM Presence" has sustained you for eons of time and desires to bring into your world the wonders of the Universe.

When the incarnated soul voluntarily disconnects itself from conscious contact with that Presence, the "I AM" continues, in graciousness and kindness, pouring its streams of Light and Life energy into your physical heart, to sustain your incarnation with the use of intelligence, emotional feeling, power of thought, memory and physical action.

Your Presence and mine are not limited in any way. They are ONE in action, in glorious perfection, all-knowing and capable of instantly directing a million or a billion rays of transcendent light into whatever condition, place or person requires assistance. Will you not raise your deep and sincere attention to that Presence and make it feel you are now ready and willing to work consciously with it again?

When you do this, your Presence will turn its attention to you, the stream of Light will widen and your capacity to serve will increase through that renewed partnership. From the heart of that Presence, you can direct those mighty rays of intelligent light, including the Violet Fire, to all life everywhere which you may have injured or been injured by. It can go back in time from the moment the shadows of human creation first began to fall upon this dear Earth. At your call, your Presence will gladly clear and balance in one hour, and perhaps in just one moment any debt you may have incurred with any lifestream, whether embodied now or not.

Transmission from the Heart of Beloved Saint Germain

Beloved children of my Heart, it is my great pleasure and privilege to contribute my messages of Love in the writing of this alchemical "Seven Sacred Flames" book. Indeed, we consider this publication to be a sacred document for the benefit of mankind. Know, dear ones, that as you read and study the material contained on each page and paragraph of this book, my presence and the presence of the other Chohans of the Seven Rays, along with those of your beloved Lemurian family of Telos, will accompany you.

You will find in these writings everything you need to know and integrate to qualify for your Ascension. If only you choose to seriously apply the wisdom herein and fully become it, letting go of all fears and preconceived ideas you have regarding your true nature, your pathway will certainly unfold with the greatest Ease and Grace. You are the ones, beloved friends, who create all the difficulties and complexities in the process of "becoming again" what you have always been.

Beloveds, realize that it is not so complicated and difficult to become an Ascended Master if only you allow yourself, without your usual resistance, to naturally "be" in the flow of your divinity. A divine being in an incarnated experience is truly what you are; it is your birthright and natural state. You have never been anything else! Allow the nudging of your beloved I AM Presence to rule your heart, to rule your life in total trust, and let go of your resistance and fears.

It is important for me to bring to your attention that we have been observing you and humanity very closely for a long time. From our perspective of Love and Limitlessness, it is obvious to all of "Us" on this side of the veil, that humanity in general, including most of those who have applied for Ascension in this life, share a common problem you are not aware of. Whether you are willing to admit it or not, the fact remains that most of you, if not all, hold a great fear of your "I AM Presence" and of embracing your divinity.

You have been relentlessly programmed over the centuries and millennia by those of the shadow side, who have ruled various aspects of your planet, to fear what you do not fully understand, and to reject or fight it. Your souls are profoundly imprinted with that erroneous signature of fear. You have also been imprinted with the belief that you are a poor sinner, not worthy of Love, and certainly not worthy to be a true "Son of God," an equal to the Christ within you now wishing to externalize. You have all been imprinted with the thoughts and feeling of unworthiness, despair and hopelessness.

Now I ask you to contemplate this state of consciousness thoroughly because it is a major obstacle to Ascension. We urge you to heal and transform that debilitating state. When you heal those parasitic imprints in your consciousness and fully recognize your true nature, it will be easy for you to perceive the wonders of your divinity and simply embrace them. You will simply step into your divinity like you do an old shoe.

I admit that to attain full healing and transformation of the former consciousness will take work, processing and forgiveness. Nevertheless, this is the healing required to pass through all the initiations of the Seven Great Temples. I repeat, "it does not have to be hard or painful." In fact, you can make a game of it, perceiving it to be the greatest adventure of all your lifetimes put together, and ride the wave of Ascension in Joy, Love, Harmony and Peace, transforming all challenges into Divine Grace. In your world, you call this "to take the lemons and make lemonade."

I see your hearts, I see the strengths and weaknesses, and I see the tenderness in each of your souls. Yet, I see and know that tomorrow's world is being built today through the consciousness of individuals WILLING to sit at the feet of the Masters and accept their words, their understanding, their promises, their visions and their truth.

Contemplate, in the silence of your own sanctuary, the power of God within you, and allow it to transform your world. I am committed to helping you, for YOU are my representatives! You are the lifestreams that mankind can see! When you dedicate yourselves in service for the benefit of humanity, your bodies, your world and consciousness represents my teachings, my world, my very self, and the self of all the masters who are assisting this planet and her evolution.

Dear ones, know that we, of the hierarchy, are dependent upon you to mirror that which you have received through the years from me and from the other Masters of this planetary Brotherhood. In the name of God and of your own I AM Presence, I say to you, "arise in the mastery of your Godhood! Allow yourself to wear the magnificent Robes of Freedom that I wish to bestow upon you as my representative in the outer world, and which you shall, in kindness and love, place upon the shoulders of men, women and children who have incarnated to be part of this wondrous Golden Age of enlightenment"! Use the power of the Sacred Fire daily! Who among you is going to arise and BE? We shall see!

To those who have looked into the future and listened to the words of the Masters who speak freely of a Golden Age that is to come, it is pleasing to the heart to hear, amusing to the mind, and gives hope to those in despair. It is your job, dear ones, to manifest that Golden Age. As masters in our realm, we have accomplished this already and live it. It is now up to you to demonstrate enough mastery to create this Age of Enlightenment that you have been waiting for.

WHEN are you going to begin to externalize this Golden Age, which is my responsibility as Chohan of the Seventh Ray, to manifest on this planet? It is to those of you who have awakened and accepted the presence of the spiritual hierarchy and the ascended masters' teachings that I look for the inception of the Golden Age upon Earth, in your lives, in your home, in your work and in your own sanctuary. You will become a powerful magnet, drawing the masses to you. And know that, at first, they will be more interested in the fruit and harvest of your endeavor than in the process by which you have attained your Victory in the Light.

We require an army of Light to bring this assignment to completion! To you who are my friends I give the assignment to initiate "now" the establishment of the Seventh Golden Age of harmony, peace, beauty, abundance, perfection and true Brotherhood, through the path of the Love of your own heart flame! Remember, every great thing had a humble beginning!

I am Saint Germain, your brother and friend. I have come to claim your soul and the fires of your heart for the victory of the Aquarian age. I have set the patterns for your soul's initiations. I AM on the path of freedom, and I AM the God of Freedom. Take that path and you will find me there. I am your teacher if you will have me. From the ashram of the great Violet Temple, along with the Violet Flame Temple of Telos and your eternal friend Adama, we send you blessings of joy through the miracles of the Violet Flame of Transformation and Freedom.

Seat of the Soul Chakra

Invocation to the Violet Flame

Mantle of Violet Fire

From the Lord God of my Being, I AM That I AM, I call to beloved Saint Germain and your legions of cosmic Violet Flame angels to come forth to infuse and saturate my being with all activities of the Sacred Fire, especially the Violet Flame of Transmutation and Freedom.

- Clothe me with your cosmic mantel of Violet Fire of Transmutation, Healing, Freedom, Diplomacy and the Science of true Alchemy.

- Dissolve and consume from my being all that does not reflect perfect Love and Harmony.

- Through Mercy's Flame, transmute all errors of the past and barriers to my Ascension.

- Protect the youth of this world in an aura of Violet Flame.

- With much gratitude, I ask this to be manifest in God's Holy name. And so be it, Beloved I AM!

(Repeat the whole invocation three times)

Discourse from Adama with Master St. Germain

Adama speaks to us about the Violet Ray, the Ray of Transmutation, accompanied by the presence of Master Saint Germain. A wonderful meditation is offered at the end instructing us how to use the Violet Flame on our personal path to mastery.

Aurelia - The Violet Ray represents the energy of change, alchemy and freedom. I would like to invite you to open yourself to a heart-to-heart communion with Adama and the Master Saint Germain. Adama is quite the heart doctor, and so is Saint Germain. As he speaks, he addresses himself directly to your heart, activating a level of healing. This is basically what Adama likes to do. He is also the one that can plug you into Telos in more ways than one.

Group - Could you explain who Saint Germain is for those not familiar with this alchemical master?

Aurelia - Saint Germain is and has been for eons the guardian of the Violet Flame. Within the Spiritual Hierarchy, he holds the position of the Chohan of the Seventh Ray. This means that he is the guardian of the Violet Flame of Freedom and Transmutation for the planet, which is the action of the Seventh Ray.

He was very well known in France, prior to and during the French revolution, as "The Count of Saint Germain." This immortal being lived, and was seen regularly by many, for over three hundred years, always maintaining the appearance of a 40-year-old man. He was called "The Wonder Man of Europe," who spoke all languages, played any and all musical instruments and demonstrated in front of his friends many activities of alchemy. He was also known as the one who would materialize in one place, dematerialize in a few moments and reappear several hundred miles away a few minutes later. He has an enjoyable sense of humor, and is exceptionally articulate, especially in the English language. Saint Germain has always been a real delight to my soul whenever I have contact or conversations with this beloved one. To just hear or mention his name makes my heart sing with gladness.

Master Saint Germain is the one who has been upholding the Flame of Freedom for the planet for over 70,000 years. He is an awesome and dedicated master in service to humanity. As the master Jesus was the Avatar of the Piscean age, Saint Germain is now stepping in for the next 2,000 years to be the Avatar of the Aquarian age. He is fully supported by Jesus/Sananda and our Lemurian family of Telos, as well as the spiritual hierarchy of this planet, this galaxy and universe. Some masters hold certain offices for a time, and then step into a new post, leaving the former post to someone with the attainment to take their place.

Group - *Was he also embodied as the great Merlin of Camelot?*

Aurelia - Oh, yes, he was Merlin in the time of Camelot in England. Merlin was a noble magician, not in the sense of playing mediocre tricks, but a great master alchemist. Unfortunately, Merlin has been depicted in so many movies and writings, by those unaware, as a wizard of some kind, with a dubious reputation. That is not the truth of who he was as Merlin. Merlin was one of the greatest alchemists of all time, and Saint Germain is one of the greatest masters who has served this planet almost since its inception.

All other masters honor him greatly for the service he has done for the planet with the Violet Flame dispensation. The Violet Flame is one of the most important flames for redemption, transmutation and freedom. It is like a fire of love that cleanses. Saint Germain said once if he were to talk about the Violet Flame for a whole month, twenty-four hours a day, seven days a week, he could not cover all its benefits. Let's hear what Adama has to say.

Adama - Good evening my beloved friends, this is Adama of Telos. Tonight, as always, I have my regular team of twelve masters with me. We also enjoy the honor of having the Master Saint Germain present with us as a participant. Though I am talking through Aurelia, the energy of Saint Germain is blended with mine. It is a great privilege for us, because Master Saint Germain is so deeply loved in the inner planes, and highly respected by everyone throughout the entire cosmos. He spends much time with us in Telos. We all work together to bring forth the energies of ascension for the planet and for humanity.

I would like to give you some explanation about the Seventh Ray and if you have questions, feel free to interrupt, so that we can create more of a dialogue.

The Violet Flame is a combination of the blue and pink ray. It is not one ray by itself. It is a combination of blue for power and pink for love, uniting the energies of the divine masculine with the divine feminine in a wondrous action of spiritual alchemy. The main role of the Violet Flame is transmutation, an alchemical term meaning to create positive change. For example, by invoking and working with the Violet Flame, you can transmute huge amounts of karma or misqualified energy from this or past incarnations.

Once the energy is transmuted, you never have to deal with it anymore in your present life, because those energies have been erased and forgiven into love and joy with the use of the Violet Fire. As you work with the energy of the Violet Ray, it radiates and dissolves unbalanced energies in your auric field, as well as your conscious, subconscious and unconscious minds. It can heal many conditions in your lives.

The Violet Flame can dissolve karma, once you have full understanding of the experiences lived and the energy patterns created. With its energies, you can also create wondrous beauty because it is composed of the power and love frequencies. Also included in the Violet Ray activity is the Flame of forgiveness and compassion, which are needed to create harmony and manifestation in your life.

There are other attributes of the Violet Flame, such as the comfort flame and the flame of diplomacy and ceremony. These are all Seventh Ray activities. Whenever you create comfort, no matter what form it takes, you engage in a Seventh Ray activity. We also call the Violet Flame, the Freedom Love Flame. When you gain spiritual freedom, you become limitless, and all the attributes of your divinity are at your command. This is total freedom, not just freedom from one thing. The Violet Flame is a vital tool for your spiritual progress and evolution.

Aurelia - *What exactly do you mean when you talk about the process of spiritual awakening? How can we begin to use the Violet Flame to heal ourselves and our lives?*

Adama - The Seventh Ray can assist in the purification of the substances and the energies of life. There are many ways you can use the Violet Flame constructively and effectively. You can use it through prayers and invocations; you can also visualize it in your meditation and set your intention to receive an infusion of this energy in all aspects of your being.

You can breathe it into every cell, atom and electron of your body. You can cleanse and purify every thought and feeling in your auric field. Be creative and start writing your own prayers and invocations to it. When these come from the fire of your own heart, they are more powerful than those that have been written by other people. Prayers written by others are most suited for those who wrote them. Work with it each day and start creating miracles of love in your lives.

Invocation to the Violet Flame

As an example, *"In the name of the I AM of my being, in the name of God, I now call forth the action of the Violet Flame of transmutation, of compassion and forgiveness in my auric field, for the cleansing and purifying of every thought and feeling in my solar plexus and in all of my chakras. I ask the action of the Violet Fire to permeate every cell, atom and electron of my four body systems at this moment and at all times each day of my life, 24 hours a day, 7 days a week for the healing of all distortions in my energy fields from past and present misunderstandings. I ask the energies of the Violet Fire to start healing all distortions in my physical, emotional and mental bodies. With much gratitude, I now ask for the action of the Violet Fire to manifest in my energy fields in full power. And so be it."*

You can use this kind of invocation or create your own. Sit quietly visualizing it, breathing it in. Using the breath in a conscious and sustained manner brings it into your auric field in a more tangible and creative manner. Then ask the Violet Flame to sustain this activity for the rest of the day, and it will continue its action for you while you perform your other daily activities. The action will continue uninterrupted as long as you remain in harmony. Whenever you invoke any flame of God and you ask for its momentum to be sustained, its activity will continue until you engage in disharmony in your feeling world. That vibration stops it until you make peace within yourself and invoke it again. As long as you stay harmonious in your thoughts and feelings, the flame will continue to work. If you come to a situation of disharmony, invoke it again to recover your emotional balance.

The more you visualize it, and the more you stay in your heart with it in your meditation, the more momentum it is building. There was a time with earlier dispensations in the last century when people were not very willing to meditate. So we formulated a series of decrees where many people invoked the Violet Flame or the flame of other rays daily, and sometimes for long hours. Unfortunately, for many people, this type of devotion became a mental ritual, lacking the real fervor of their hearts.

Though these people meant well and were sincere, it is best to say a decree or prayer only a few times with all the fervor that the heart can muster, and take the time needed to create the alchemy of love. When you make an invocation or prayer, allow yourself to fully feel its energy in your heart and charge it with love; then allow the energy to do its perfect work.

There are several thousand people in the last century who made their ascension by invoking the Violet Flame every day for years and years. They invoked it with much love and fervor in their hearts without ever really knowing what they were transmuting. They allowed all their shadows to surface to their awareness, without ever judging them, but surrendered the energies by bathing them in the Violet Fire.

These dear souls did not have access to all the tools and information you now have. It was through faith and consistency that they continued until they could breathe their last human breath. By this gradual process, they changed, little by little, all the negative energy from many lives, past and present, into pure golden liquid light. When they passed on to the other side of the veil, they made their glorious ascension without delay.

Today, they are among us, wearing robes of Light and enjoying all the bounty of the fifth dimension.

Aurelia - *Do you have to be consciously aware of what you are transmuting?*

Adama - Not always. It is good to know in some cases, but it is not a requirement. What is important is that you pour your love into it. It is always the love, the forgiveness and the compassion poured into a situation that transmutes it into something better, by changing a negative situation into a positive one, and by gaining the wisdom those energies are trying to teach you. If you have a problem with someone, send waves and waves of Violet Flame to him or her. As you send waves of love, compassion, forgiveness and blessing to a situation, it becomes impossible for it to remain the same; universal law requires resolution for whatever receives love and blessings.

The activity of blessing is also a form of transmutation, a Seventh Ray activity.

As you start blessing all that manifests as less than divine perfection in your lives, you are transforming or transmuting situations that appear to be negative into something far more positive; you create the divine solution, and the win-win situation for everyone manifests. This is what transmutation does; it creates a transformation that makes everyone a winner.

Aurelia - *How would someone having a problem with their spouse, or ill feelings toward their boss or anyone else use the Violet Flame to transmute or heal their situation?*

Adama - First of all, you have to be detached from the outcome. If you start out wanting to make changes or desiring a specific outcome, you will most likely miss the boat. This is why it is always wiser to ask for the perfect divine solution. If you desire to be specific about the outcome you wish to create, it is important that you "allow" the space for a different outcome by adding to your prayer or intention: "this or something better, according to the divine will." Your higher self sees and knows the bigger picture that is veiled from you. Let's say a marriage situation appears to be ending. At the time you say, "Oh, my gosh! I prayed and I invoked so much Violet Flame into that situation, I did all I could to be loving, compassionate and to bring resolution with love and forgiveness, and now it seems I have a more challenging situation."

Now contemplate this; ask yourself if the ending of a marriage was a failure or a spiritual victory. I say that if you have done your very best, and a situation does not end the way you hoped for, perhaps it was a karmic relationship that had reached completion. Perhaps your higher self is now ready to open your life to something much more appropriate for your pathway and for your happiness. The marriage break-up in that case was certainly a spiritual success, not a failure. Because of the fine quality of inner work that was done, the right to move on to something more fulfilling is earned. The feeling of the loss or sense of failure is but a temporary human illusion.

Two years later, you find yourself in a wondrous new relationship, where you are so much happier and where there is so much more affinity and harmony. Will you remember at the time the pool of Violet Fire you previously invoked that created this new avenue in your life? There are times when karmic situations are resolved and it is time to move on. This is the way your prayers are answered; you are now "free" to experience something better, versus staying in a relationship that has reached completion. At this time, it is important to let go of situations that no longer serve you. The divine solution may not always, at first, appear to be what you want, but whatever is created will always be for your spiritual advancement, and will always bring the best result. The Violet Flame is also known as the "miracle worker."

When you bless the person you have a problem with, a spouse or neighbor, or your boss or someone in your work environment, or a relative, visualize her/him bathing in the love vibration of the Violet Flame. Acknowledge the right of that person to become free of his/her own burdens, and awaken to their full potential. Do this with compassion and forgiveness. Also use the flame of diplomacy in all your interactions with others; this is part of the Seventh Ray activity. If you start using the Seventh Ray with its many attributes, and have no personal agenda other than wanting the best outcome of the divine will, you will be amazed at the miracles that can manifest in your own lives and in the lives of others around you. This is how peace on earth will be created.

Aurelia - *Many people are going to find the part about not having a personal agenda difficult, because they want it their own way.*

Adama - Most of you are so focused on the end results of what you want that you tend to lose sight of what you have to release in order to let go and let the God within do its perfect work. The various flames of God contain divine intelligence or consciousness. They are aware of the bigger picture and they know what is best for you. There are literally hundreds of thousands and millions of guardians and masters working with each flame.

Wanting it your way is like saying, "Well God, I want this, but I want it my way, even if it is ultimately not for my greatest good." If you insist, do not be surprised if you get it. God always wants to give you the desires of your heart, and you may soon find out that this is not really what you needed. These flames want to bring forth the most magnificent outcomes in your life, but what you are determined to have is what will manifest. When you are determined to have it your own way, the universe will give it to you and you may find out several months or years later that you missed a better outcome. Remember, lack of trust was the energy of the original fall of consciousness of mankind, and the experiences you had with that lack of trust have been very painful indeed. This need to always be in charge, instead of being "in allowance" has created much disharmony. The higher aspect of "You" loves you totally and wants nothing but your happiness and to bring you back home to enlightenment and mastery.

People are afraid to experience the dark night of their own creation. What got people in trouble in the first place was this lack of trust. When people decided they no longer wished to trust God to feed them three times a day, and decided to get their own meals, a misalignment was created. When they stopped listening to the voice of their own spirit, they separated themselves from the flow of the Divine. Now, several thousand lifetimes later, there is no longer trust in the union between Divine Spirit and Will, and nearly everyone lives in fear and lack of some kind. Now, it is your time, through experience and acceptance, to regain and relearn the energy of trust, in spite of appearances. Through intention and release, through allowance of all that is, the "boulders" you have created that block the "Door of Everything" will be dissolved, and you will be free to "step in." You will finally be home!

Aurelia - Is this the bottom line with the healing that is needed to take place in all of our hearts and souls?

Adama - Exactly. Soon, humanity is going to begin learning their lessons in more dramatic ways. Events will transpire on the planet requiring people make the biggest choices of many lifetimes. Your Earth Mother will soon no longer tolerate the type of separation that has transpired here on Her body, and people are going to have to shape up or ship out. The new world order for this planet is not what your world leaders are projecting, but will be a life in total union with the Presence of the God-within and with the Creator. Divine order will be restored here in a few short years.

Events that appear to be unjust or unfair are usually mirrors of the consciousness of the people. They are always created with the energies of the collective consciousness. For example, in your country many people do not like your government, and do not want to become involved in any political activity because it is perceived as "too negative." You have books upon books, websites upon websites, describing all the wrongs and the corruption of your government.

What is written and presented to the public is usually true, and though your governments are corrupt to the very core, you need to remember that they always mirror the "consciousness" of the people they govern. What does that tell you? When the people collectively raise their consciousness to embrace universal laws of love, truth and harmony, they no longer attract the kind of government you now have. This is not only in the USA but also applies to all countries on this planet. When a cataclysm occurs, the same holds true. Cataclysms are nothing more than nature's way of cleansing the imbalances and toxicity created by the consciousness of the collective. You do not honor the earth, you trash her body, you create increasingly more pollution and you use her resources unwisely. In so doing as a collective, you create large pools of unbalanced energies that sooner or later must be released and cleansed by the cataclysms you often experience in various places on the planet.

When these balancing cataclysms manifest, they are charged with wave upon wave of Violet Flame, full of God's fire that purifies. After a war, there is a tremendous amount of personal and planetary karma balanced. Greater understanding is reached, although it may not seem apparent when this truth is viewed through the eyes of those who still strive to control your free will. True, many people have suffered, but they also balanced their own personal karma in the process. After World War II, when so much karma was balanced on the planet, it opened the way for the expansion, new technology and greater ease you enjoy today.

Aurelia - *Do you mean that everything we experience in our personal relationships, or as a society, a culture and country, are all mirrors created to reflect self and the collective consciousness?*

Adama - Everything that happens, be it on a personal or global level, whether it is a volcano erupting, an earthquake, a riot in one of your cities or a war, always reflects the unbalanced or repressed energy the people are holding within themselves. It reflects the anger, the fears, the deceptions, the greed, the human injustices, the grief, etc., that people are holding within their souls. They are nothing more than mirrors of what is out of alignment at the human level.

Aurelia - *Most people do not understand how we create our reality. They say that if they created their own reality, they would create the perfect body, house or mate, abundant money, etc.*

Adama - The problem is that people have not yet understood or realized how they are creating. Also, their creation does not necessary stem from this lifetime alone; "karma" or lack of understanding has to be cleared before the new and perfect can be manifested. People create constantly with their moment-by-moment thoughts and feelings, their words and actions, and the internal dialogues in the mind during every waking hour. People may say, I want the perfect body or marriage, but the thoughts and feelings they entertain most of the time do not support their desires. If someone were to show them, moment-by-moment, what their thoughts and feelings are, and how unbalanced they are in creating their reality, they would understand why they do not have the healthy or perfect body they desire, or the perfect relationship and abundance they want.

People have to really become conscious of their thoughts, feelings, words and actions. Words are very powerful, and you constantly reinforce their energy with your feelings. Yet words do not always match your feelings. You may say I want more money, but inside you feel poor. You want to be involved in a better relationship, but inside you feel you do not deserve it and you are not willing to weed out the garden of your soul in order to attract that perfect mate. You say, I want a perfect body, but inside you do not love yourself. You do not love your body as it is, and you are not in acceptance of the lessons you are learning with your body in its present form.

The body can only respond to love, and nearly all of you do not love or take care of that body of yours like we do in Telos. Very few of you love yourself enough to nurture yourself and your body properly and consistently. Most of you do not give your body the proper nourishment it needs to rejuvenate and radiate perfect health. How then do you expect to create a perfect body for yourself? You constantly reaffirm what you do not want instead of what you want.

You live in a house of mirrors, and the universe gives you back much of what you create through your thoughts, feelings and words. When you decree "I am sick and tired of this and of that," you are creating very powerful affirmations that return to you the energies you just named. You are constantly creating affirmations of what you don't want. Be aware that the universe hears you and honors what you say. "If she says she is sick and tired, and keeps affirming it with so much strength and power, it must be what she wants. Let's give it to her or him." And so you get more of the same, and the mirrors keep reflecting.

Aurelia - *Now in terms of using the Violet Flame to balance karma, since we obviously still have to learn the lessons from the karma, how do we learn the lesson if we simply use the Violet Flame to get rid of it?*

The Violet Flame will not "just get rid of it." That is not its purpose. The Violet Flame will assist in balancing it, but it will teach you as well the lessons you need to learn, albeit in a more gentle way. If you remain in resistance to the lessons and understanding that your challenging situations teach you, the use of the Violet Flame may not bring the desired results. It cannot be misused to prevent you from gaining the experience and wisdom that are ultimately the true meaning of karma.

Yet there is a difference between learning a lesson in a gentle way, from wise guidance that you embrace, to living through a very difficult experience in order to receive the same understanding. Do you see the difference? The Violet Flame can bring you to a space where you learn your lessons in a very loving and gentle manner, where you can learn in ease and grace. It does not have to be as painful or difficult as what you are choosing to experience with your lessons at this time. Your resistance to open yourself to the higher and easier ways is what creates the harshness in your lives.

Another Invocation to the Violet Flame: Here is another way you can use the Violet Flame for the world around you. You can definitely make an invocation and say: *"In the name of the great I AM, I call to beloved* Saint Germain, *to saturate the world with waves upon waves of Violet Fire, to infuse every particle of life, every man, woman and child on this planet in an auric field of*

Violet Flame to protect and to awaken them. I ask that this action be sustained until perfection is restored. And so be it."

You can make this invocation in your daily prayers and call on the millions of Violet Flame angels who are just waiting for your petition to go to work. Send them everywhere to fill the world with Violet Fire. Angels are not allowed to interfere in your world unless the call is made from your plane. Send them to work; they are waiting to answer your prayers. The Violet Flame angels can literally flood the planet with Violet Fire and reduce much pain. In your daily life, ask them to flood your personal world with the Violet Flame energy.

Aurelia - *It seems important to send the energy of that flame out to every man, woman and child on the planet, and with our hearts, flood the earth with that energy.*

Adama - Yes, and don't forget the animals, the trees, the elementals, the nature spirits and the plant kingdom. The elementals are often in need of your assistance, your love, your support and your invocations to the Violet Flame, in order to be able to maintain balance on the planet. They need it now more than ever during this time of transition. The elementals are very involved with assisting the planet into the higher octave; they are your helpers. The more Violet Flame and love they receive from humanity, the smoother the transition is going to be for the Earth and for all kingdoms living on her body.

Aurelia - *Adama, do the Lemurians use the Violet Flame in Telos to maintain the level of perfection you all experience there?*

Adama - You bet we do. We use the energies of the Violet Flame constantly. In various temples, the energies of the sacred fires are perpetually invoked by the members of the priesthood and by the people of our community. In our main temple, the temple of Ma-Ra, we have consecrated an area to each one of the seven flames. Our people take turns tending and nurturing those flames around the clock. We live in the consciousness of those flames, and we constantly embrace their full energies. In turn, we are blessed beyond measure by Life.

Outside of Telos, in the area of the etheric Lemurian City of Light, we have temples consecrated for each one of the main sacred flames. These temples are quite large and the beings living in these areas nurture these flames with their love, devotion and invocations around the clock. The fifth dimensional population is quite large; the masters and angels of the sacred fire, along with the priesthood of these temples, take turns tending and invoking the qualities and attributes of these flames. They do so for themselves, for the planet, for humanity and for the energy required to maintain and increase the level of perfection of the dimension they live in.

This type of ritual, dear ones, is done in every dimension. Angels of the sacred fires and angels from various choirs join in support of the many flames we nurture, and this is what makes the higher dimensions so beautiful and wondrous to live in. This activity was also carried forth in all temples in the time of Lemuria, Atlantis, Egypt and in all former golden ages.

It will soon become important that on the surface, you start becoming involved with the nurturing and expansion of these flames, first within yourself and for the planet. We have done this for ourselves, but also on your behalf for centuries. Soon, it will be required that those on the surface who aspire to ascend, step into more spiritual maturity. You will be required to bring your own personal contribution to these flames for humanity and for the planet. It is a requirement in the fifth dimension. Are you ready for a meditation now?

Meditation

Journey to the Violet Flame Temple in Telos

With Adama and Master Saint Germain

I now ask that you center in your heart and state your intention to be filled with the loving energies of your divine presence. You may do this in this manner: *"In the name of the I AM that I AM, from the Lord God of my being, I ask now that every cell, every atom and every electron of my four body systems, all my subtle bodies, every particle of life of who I am in all dimensions and states of consciousness, be totally filled with the wonders and the miracle energies of the Violet Flame of Freedom's Love. I now ask to be filled again and again, twenty-four hours a day, each day of my life." (Breathe it in.)*

As you are being filled with the Violet Flame energies, set your intentions to come on a journey with us and with your higher self to the beautiful Violet Flame Temple in the fifth dimension inside Telos. This temple has an etheric physical structure, and our people can access it any time; and so can you in your light body. In this temple, the Violet Flame burns perpetually, nurtured by the love and devotion of our people, blessing life, blessing mankind and the planet. This is a place where Master Saint Germain spends much time with his twin flame Portia and with legions of Violet Flame angels, recharging and tending the energies of the Violet Flame for the planet.

Keep breathing the energy as much as you can, so that you can bring it back with you to your physical body when you return to full consciousness. Now, see yourself standing in a large circular room with a high ceilings, where the Violet Flame is present everywhere. The walls are made of pure violet amethyst and the floor is also made of amethyst crystal of a smoother texture and lighter color. Piercing through the amethyst wall you see a great number of violet-tone lights that give you the feeling of a mystical starry vision. The room is bright and you see dozens of fountains of all sizes and shapes emitting every possible shade of violet hue in a magical play of colors and tones.

The water fairies have great fun playing with these energies; watch their exultation in their playful joy. The flower fairies are busy creating beautiful flowers of all shades of white, gold and violet with this light energy. See them throwing some at you, as their way of blessing and welcoming you. Join in to partake of their joy and bliss. Also notice the multitudes of Violet Flame angels tending the Violet Fire with their love and adoration.

The Violet Fire is not hot; it is basically on the cool side. There are several chairs in the room, and we ask each of you to choose the one you are drawn to, where it feels the most comfortable to you. The chairs are made of pure violet crystal, and under each one is a flame of violet rising up to enfold you. As it burns up from underneath, it is entering and infusing every part of your body through the lower chakras. There is also another flame coming down from above penetrating your crown chakra and infusing every cell of your body.

As you breathe it into your heart consciously, you are being filled with the Violet Flame of Freedom like never before. There are several Violet Flame angels surrounding each one of you, pouring cups of love and cups of Violet fire into your energy fields and the various aspects of your life needing healing. The experience is going to be different for each one of you. Keep breathing in the energy. Now see the Master St. Germain with his Lady Portia and the Lady Kuan Yin, the Goddess of Mercy and Compassion, filling you with their love and imprinting your auric field with the flame of compassion, which is also a Seventh Ray energy.

Now open yourself to a greater level of compassion for your own healing and for the healing of those you love. Whatever it is that you feel needs healing in your life, invoke the energies of compassion and forgiveness into it, and allow the changes you want to take place. Stay in that state of bliss as long as you want. Talk to us, talk to Saint Germain or Kuan Yin, and set your intentions to completely heal yourself, to heal all traumas of the present and the past. This room is filled with powerful healing energy, and as you sit and bathe in it, feel dark energy transformed into Light. Wherever there have been problems, trauma or pain, feel the energy starting to lift and dissolve.

Feel a lessening of density and how much lighter you are becoming. Feel the lightness and the sensation of joy infusing your being. As you allow yourself to feel greater joy, you lessen your burdens. Allow this lightness, this beauty, this love and power to nurture you. Keep breathing it in. Consciously request of the Violet Flame what you would like it to do for you. Sometimes, between your asking and the fulfillment of your request, clearing processes need to take place, but step-by-step you are working towards your victory. Do not feel rushed; take all the time you need.

When you feel ready, you look around and see guides, masters and angels smiling at you, willing to assist you if you have a query. The angels, by the way, especially those who work with mankind, come here to recharge with the Violet Flame vibration several times a week and often daily. The unbalanced energy on the planet contaminates their forcefield, and they come here to cleanse and revitalize. We invite you to do the same. Stay with us here as long as you wish, and when you are ready, come back to full consciousness. Now be mindful of not re-creating in your lives through your thoughts, feelings and words the energies you have just transmuted.

The Seventh Ray

We invite you to come back to this temple any time you want. The door is now opened to you. Master Saint Germain will often be there for you and his angels will delight in offering their love and assistance.

As we conclude our talk this day, we honor you for your openness. We send you blessings of love, courage and wisdom. We will also join our dear friend Saint Germain who commits to sending waves of Violet Flame into the hearts of all those who will be reading this material later on. And so be it.

Prayer Section

Invocations to the Seven Sacred Flames for Personal and Planetary Healing and Transformation

Formulate these prayers once, three times, six times or nine times for each one, according to your inner guidance. Each time you repeat a prayer, you build a momentum of Light encoded in the prayer.

Prayer Section

Prayers and Invocations to the First Ray Royal Blue Flame of God's Will

The Prayer of Surrender

By Master El Morya

Beloved Father/Mother God, into Thy hands I commend my being. Use my love, my thoughts and my life in selfless service to Thee. Release from me all that hinders the fulfillment of my holy purposes and Ascension. Teach me to be kind in the ways of the Brotherhood of Light. Direct and establish my lifestream in ways that, daily and hourly, my true identity in God manifests.

> Beloved God-Presence I AM, Eternal Father/Mother God,
> May the covenant I made with Thee be totally fulfilled!
> May I live my life to feel Your Love and see Your Light!
> May your Will manifest on Earth as it is in Heaven!
> Into thy hands I surrender my being, that through me,
> God be glorified in all things! And so be it! Beloved I AM.

For a Forcefield of Protection

Light is the most powerful emanation of all Creation. It is important to invoke the full Power of God's First Ray for Protection and Divine Will.

In the name of my beloved I AM Presence, from the very Heart of God, I invoke an invincible shaft of God's First Ray of Protection to be placed over me. Let it surround every cell, atom and electron of my Being, encapsulating me in an invincible forcefield of God's Holy Will. Let this shaft of Sapphire Blue Light expand into my various bodies and all my chakras.

Cut me FREE from anything that is less than the highest Light within me. Let the Blue Flame of Divine Love guard my forcefield of Protection, daily and hourly. I know that "I AM" absolutely protected at all time and in all places. I express my deep gratitude for all assistance given unto me always. Amen

Prayer Section

Prayers and Invocations to the Second Ray Golden Yellow Flame of Illumination

Call to the Illumination Flame

Illumination Flame from the Heart of God
Expand thy Light through me always
Golden Flame from the Heart of God
Fill my heart with thy Wisdom Ray
Illumination Flame from the Heart of God
Expand God's Mind through all my thoughts
Golden Flame from the Heart of God
Illumine the Earth with thy Golden Light
Golden Flame from the Heart of God
To thy Love and Light I bow! (3X)

Invocation to the Sun

Father/Mother Light of our Solar System

Helios and Vesta! Helios and Vesta! Helios and Vesta!
Let your Golden Light flow within every part of my being!
Let your Golden Light expand within my Sacred Heart!
Let your Golden Light spread throughout the Earth!
Let the Earth ascend into Her glorious Destiny!
And let me ascend into my glorious Ascension. (3X)

The Seven Sacred Flames

Prayers and Invocations to the Third Ray Rose-Pink Flame of Cosmic Love

Adoration to Your God Presence

Beloved Great Presence, I AM,
Thou Life that beats my heart,
Blaze now thy radiant Love Rays.
Let me be an anchor of Love for all.
Flood me with Thy Glory and
Let my heart be always with You.

My beloved God Presence, I AM
I invoke thy great Radiance
Infuse my mind and heart with Thy Love
Expand and raise my consciousness
To Ascended Masters' octave of Light
With all Your Love, with all Your Love
Merge with me more and more each day,
Until I become Thyself in manifestation.

I AM, I AM adoring Thee, (3X)
In deep gratitude, I offer my love to Thee (2X)
Love me, love me, love me. (2X)
Beloved I AM, Beloved I AM, Beloved I AM!

Prayer Section

Prayer for Divine Love

In the Name of my Beloved I AM Presence
I call the Power of Divine Love to be magnified
within my heart and world daily.
I AM Love, Joyous Love
Radiating Love, Unconditional Love!
God consumes my shadows
Transmuting them into Love!

This day, I AM a focus of Divine Love
Flowing through every cell of my being!
I AM a living stream of pure Divine Love
That can never be re-qualified by fear,
Anger, hatred, dislikes and greed!
All negative thoughts and feelings
Are NOW dissolved and consumed
By the power of Divine Love which I AM!

I AM, I AM, I AM Love,
I live in the consciousness of Love!
I AM Love in its fullest expression,
Blessing all mankind with Divine Love!
I radiate love! I AM Love in action
Blessing, Uplifting and Healing all on Earth!

The Seven Sacred Flames

Prayers and Invocations to the Fourth Ray Dazzling White Ascension Flame

Prayer for Self-Love and for Ascension

From the Lord God of my Being, I AM That I AM, I decree:
I have Love for my journey into my Ascension.
I have Compassion for all physical and emotional pain
I still need to heal.
I give thanks that I am now healing the past
and resurrecting the new.
As a Master of Divine expression, walking the Earth,
I now turn on the Light on my Divinity.
I now activate and transform my DNA
to its fifth dimensional potential.
I now choose to completely heal and rejuvenate
my physical body.
I choose to remain happy, harmonious and grateful.
I claim the mastery that is mine to manifest my freedom.
I allow my Divinity to manifest in a most wondrous way.
I give thanks that it is done according to God's Holy Will!
I call for shafts of Ascension Light to blaze through me
daily and hourly.
And so be it, beloved I AM!
(Repeat 3 times)

Prayer Section

Ascension Affirmations

by Archangel Gabriel

I AM a fountain of Youth and Eternal Purity
I AM the fullness of my Christ Victory
I AM one with the Heart of God
I AM the Purity of Love
I AM the Purity of the Resurrection Flame
I AM the Purity of the Healing Flame
I AM the Purity of the Ascension Flame
I AM the Purity of all my desires
I AM the Purity of all my thoughts and feelings
I AM the Purity of my intentions
I AM the Purity of all my chakras
I AM the Purity of Love in physical form
I AM God in action in all I do
I AM the fulfillment of my Ascension in the Light
I claim my Freedom and Victory in the Light NOW!
(Repeat each affirmation 3 times)

Prayers and Invocations to the Fifth Ray Emerald Green Flame of Healing

Healing Through Releasing Negative Energies

I am a Master of Divine Expression. I now release all separation and limitations that no longer serve my path of Light. I release all vows of poverty and limitations that I ever made in this and past incarnations. I release all imprints, implants, negative thought forms, black magic spells and curses, negative patterns of the human ego, illness and disease patterns and all energies that no longer serve my path of Light.

By the intervention of Divine Grace, with my full intent, I choose to release all energies of separation, limitations and all blockages back to the Universe. I ask for these energies be purified and transformed into the highest form of Light."

I invoke the assistance of the Angelic Realms, Master Hilarion, Mother Mary, Archangel Raphael, my Monad and all Ascended Masters to release from my being and world, all levels of energies that are less than my Divine Blueprint of Perfection and my Eternal Victory in the Light through my Ascension. And so be it, beloved I AM!

Prayer Section

Prayer to Request Miracles

Claim a healing miracle in your Life!

In the name of the Light of God that never fails
I accept a healing miracle in my life this day.
I claim a miracle in every level of my being.
I claim a miracle of Love for my full Resurrection.
Beloved Father/Mother God
Blaze forth your miracle of Light now.
Infuse your miracle of Light on Earth now.
I call for an Ascended Master healing miracle
In my heart, in my chakras and in my DNA.
Blaze forth the miracle Light of the Seven Rays
Blaze forth the miracle Light of the Holy Spirit
Everywhere in my being where healing is needed.
I declare that I AM a miracle of God this day.
I AM a miracle in action made manifest.
I AM a blazing miracle Light from the Great Central Sun
Resurrecting me back to my true identity in God.
Blaze the miracles of Light through,
  Beloved I AM, Beloved I AM, Beloved I AM!
(Repeat three times)

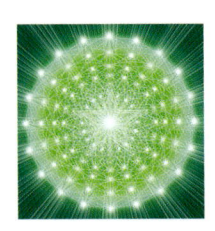

I Now Accept My Abundance

In the name of my beloved I AM Presence and my beloved Holy Christ Self, I call to the Lords of Manifestation, Angels of Prosperity, Fortuna, Goddess of Supply and Lord of Gold to assist me now in mastering all outer conditions of my life in God's perfect way, including my true abundance.

Charge! Charge! Charge into my life and use today all the blessings that are mine to receive. Infuse me with Ascended Master Wisdom and Purity that I may never again experience lack or limitation. Blaze your Heart Flame through my four body systems and expand without limit a great flow of divine abundance. Saturate me with enough Violet Flame and Emerald Healing Light to keep my life in perfect balance and harmony.

I demand God's invincible Protection and Wisdom in all my financial endeavors. I demand to become a magnet of attraction, drawing to me all the wealth that I require to fulfill my divine plan on Earth, to make my Ascension and to assist my fellowmen to do likewise. I give thanks that it is done according to God's Holy Will. I accept my abundance now with Love and Gratitude. Amen! Amen! Amen!

Gratitude is the key to attract greater abundance. Always show gratitude for everything you receive. Appreciate the wondrous assistance that we are now receiving from the Realms of Light. May you be God Victorious in all you do!

Prayer Section

Prayers and Invocations to the Sixth Ray Golden Orange Flame of Resurrection

Resurrection Affirmation

Say: "I AM the Resurrection and the Life" three times, adding to this affirmation whatever sentence you wish to specify what you want to resurrect, such as:

I AM the Resurrection and the Life of my perfect health.
I AM the Resurrection and the Life of my finances.
I AM the Resurrection and the Life of the gifts of my divinity.
I AM the Resurrection and the Life of my eternal youth & beauty.
I AM the Resurrection and the Life of my perfect work.
I AM the Resurrection and the Life of my heart flame.
I AM the Resurrection and the Life of my perfect vision.
I AM the Resurrection and the Life of my perfect relationship.

The sky is the limit, add some of your own and be creative!

Prayer of Saint Francis

LORD, make me an instrument of Your peace.
Where there is hatred, let me sow love.
Where there is injury, pardon,
Where there is doubt, faith,
Where there is despair, hope,
Where there is darkness, light,
And where there is sadness, joy.

DIVINE MASTER, grant that I may not seek
So much to be consoled as to console,
To be understood as to understand,
To be loved as to love.
For it is in giving that we receive,
In pardoning that we are pardoned,
And in dying that we are born to eternal life.

**Say it each day three times and expect
a miracle of transformation!**

Prayer Section

Prayers and Invocations to the Seventh Ray Royal Violet Flame of Transmutation

Invocation to the Violet Flame

In the name of I AM That I AM, I now call for the action of the Violet Transmuting Flame to be activated within my entire consciousness, being and world.

> Violet Fire from the Heart of God *(3x)*
> Expand thy Light through me each day. *(3x)*
> Transmute and heal my human imperfections into the shining Diamond of God's heart and Christ Perfection.

As I surrender to Thy Radiant Light, take dominion over my life. Blaze into action the Mercy's Flame of the compassionate heart. Expand and saturate within me the wonders of the Violet Light until I AM totally transformed. Beloved I AM Presence send the Violet Flame to purify every cell, atom and electron of my being until I AM raised into my Eternal Victory by the action of the Violet Fire and the Ascension Flame. And so it is, beloved I AM!

Flood the Earth with Violet Fire

In the name of the Great I AM, I call for the Light of a thousand suns from the Great Central Sun, Angels of Violet Fire, Beloved Saint Germain, Beloved Zadkiel and Holy Amethyst, Omri Tas, ruler of the Violet planet.

In the name of God, I AM That I AM! Saturate the Earth and all of Her evolution with limitless waves of Violet Fire. I call for the action of the Violet Transmuting Flame and the action of the Will of God to manifest on Earth, now and forever, an ever increasing spiral of Divine Perfection. I call for all discord and activities on Earth that are not reflecting the highest Light and God's Holy Purposes to be miraculously swept and transformed, by the power of the Violet Flame, into Divine Love and Harmony for the restoration of Earth and Her people into their original blueprint of perfection that was originally intended.

Violet Flame! Violet Flame! O Violet Flame! In the name of God, flood the Earth, Her people and all Her kingdoms with oceans and oceans of Violet Fire until every particle of Life is restored to Divine Perfection. May Peace and Love be spread throughout the Earth! May the Earth abide in the aura of Perfect Love!

May the Earth abide in an aura of Peace, Love and Freedom! I give thanks that it is done now according to God's Holy Will! And so be it, Beloved I AM.

About Aurelia Louise Jones

Aurelia Louise Jones was born in Montreal in a French Canadian family in the early 1940's. She graduated as a nurse in the early part of her working career, and worked as a Health Counselor most of her adult life, as a naturopath and a homeopath, using various holistic modalities. She moved to the USA in 1989.

Under the sponsorship of the Brotherhood of Light and the order of Melchizedek, she was ordained as a minister in 1998. She devotes most of her time to her spiritual ministry ever since. In her role as a spiritual teacher of higher consciousness, her main focus is to awaken the consciousness of humanity to the spiritual truths leading to Ascension.

In 1997, while living in Montana, she received direct guidance from Adama and the Lemurian Council of Light of Telos to move to Mount Shasta in preparation for the fulfillment of her work with them, which has become the major expression of her life. She moved to Mount Shasta one year later in June 1998.

She is the founder and owner of Mount Shasta Light Publishing and The Lemurian Connection Network. At the request of Lady Kuan Yin, Aurelia Louise channeled through her cat Angelo a touching message from the animal kingdom, now in booklet form called: *"Angelo's Message to the World."* Angelo is her favorite cat who incarnated to be with her in order to bring his message on behalf of the animal kingdom.

She published the Telos books series, Volume 1, 2, & 3, and now *"The Seven Sacred Flames,"* bringing the Lemurian teachings to the surface population. The Telos series publications are published in many countries and in several languages.

The content of the books carry important tools for the understanding of our future on the planet and how life is really meant to be lived, and how we can change our present reality to a world of love and Light.

Aurelia Louise channels Adama, the high priest of the Lemurian city of Telos as well as other spiritual Masters of Light as part of her mission. She holds Lemurian gatherings from time to time and facilitates initiatic journeys in the Mount Shasta area in the summer time. She also holds conferences and workshops in various countries of the world.

Note from Aurelia Louise Jones

Please take note that I receive each day a large number of mail from all over the planet. It has literally become impossible for me to answer even a small percentage of this amount of mail, and be able to do the work that is assigned to me each day, to write and publish the Lemurian teachings for the expansion of my mission and tend my personal obligations.

I read your letters and would like to answer your heartfelt communications. Your love is received and appreciated, but it is not feasible for me to answer over 100 personal letters each week. I ask for your understanding and compassion.

May peace and love be with you!

Telos World-Wide Foundation

Mission

We are a non-profit organization dedicated to the expansion of the information and teachings coming from Telos in preparation for the eventual emergence of our Lemurian brothers and sisters to come forth to the surface and teach us a new way of enlighten living.

Goals

The Foundation goals are the following:
- To promote the expansion of the Lemurian mission in Canada and worldwide,
- To support the writings and work of Telos,
- To assist other groups, especially international groups, to structure themselves to promote the teachings of Telos,
- To build a center for teachings and brotherhood, and
- To raise funds to meet our goals.

Address: Telos World-Wide Foundation, Inc.
Center 7400
7400 St. Laurent, Office 226
Montreal, QU - H2R 2Y1 - CANADA
Phone: (001 Intl.) 1-514-940-7746

E-mail: info@fondationtelosintl.com or
info@telosmondiale.com
fondation@lemurianconnection.com

Web Sites: http://www.fondationtelosintl.com or
http://www.telosmondiale.com/index.php

Telos-France
Gaston Tempelmann, president
http://www.telos-france.com

Mount Shasta Light Publishing Publications

The Seven Sacred Flames..$39.00

Seven Flames Prayer Booklet $7.00

Ascension Activation Booklet $7.00

Telos – Volume 1 "Revelations of the New Lemuria" $18.00

Telos – Volume 2 "Messages for the Enlightenment of a Humanity in Transformation" $18.00

Telos – Volume 3 "Protocols of the Fifth Dimension"......$20.00

The Effects of Recreational Drugs
on Spiritual Development $4.00

Angelo's Message – "Angelo, the Angel Cat Speaks to all People on this Planet regarding the Treatment of Animals by Humanity" $8.00

These publications can be purchased:
- Directly from us by phone or mail to P.O. mailing address
- From our secure shopping cart on our web site: https://www.mslpublishing.com
- From Amazon.com
- Book stores through New Leaf book distributing

If ordering by mail, CA residents, please include 7.25% sales tax. Also include shipping charges: Priority or Media mail, according to weight and distance.

Mount Shasta Light Publishing
P.O. Box 1509, Mount Shasta, CA 96067-1509
Phone: 530-926-4599
(If no answer, leave a message)